Anonymous

Spelling and Dictation Class-Book

With etymological Exercises

Anonymous

Spelling and Dictation Class-Book
With etymological Exercises

ISBN/EAN: 9783337178260

Printed in Europe, USA, Canada, Australia, Japan

Cover: Foto ©Paul-Georg Meister /pixelio.de

More available books at **www.hansebooks.com**

Constable's Educational Series.

SPELLING AND DICTATION CLASS-BOOK.

WITH ETYMOLOGICAL EXERCISES.

EDINBURGH:
THOMAS LAURIE, COCKBURN STREET.
LONDON: SIMPKIN, MARSHALL, AND CO.; AND
HAMILTON, ADAMS, AND CO.

PREFACE.

The compiler of this Class-book has aimed above all things at *judicious omission*. He has had in view the collecting together in a classified form of all the more difficult words *in common use*. Words difficult, but rarely met with by the ordinary reader, are better learned as they occur in the course of reading, and after the pupil has obtained an accurate knowledge of the great mass of words that occur in daily conversation, in newspapers and in current literature.

It is presumed that the pupil, into whose hands this book is put, has already been accustomed to spell from his daily lessons for some years, and also to write simple sentences from dictation. He will find here a revisal of the knowledge acquired, and a test and extension of it.

The Spelling Rules have been reduced to three.

The dictation-exercises in this book have been so constructed as to convey knowledge as well as to teach spelling.

The pupil is understood to learn the columns of words by heart as a home-task, and to copy on his slate, either at home or during school-hours, the dictation-exercises,—writing them afterwards from the dictation of the master. Writing from dictation will be successfully taught only when *the preparation of dictation lessons* becomes a home-task.

Masters will find that a dictation-book of this kind will afford much better material for the daily *writing-*lessons than the wearisome and unmeaning repetition of words commonly found in copy-books. As soon as a scholar can write small text fairly, his copy should frequently at least, if not always, be a portion of his dictation-book. In this way he will not only gain a more sure and rapid mastery over the art of writing, but he will learn other things at the same time.

It is scarcely necessary to apologize for the etymological portion of the volume, as a knowledge of prefixes and affixes have a close connexion with accurate and intelligent spelling. The compiler has, except in this one respect, carefully avoided the almost universal error of confounding a spelling-book proper with either a reading-book on the one hand, or a bad dictionary of significations on the other.

CONTENTS.

	PAGE
PREFACE, ...	iii

FIRST PART.

SECTION I.
    Difficult Monosyllables, and Exercises on them, . . 7

SECTION II.
    Spelling Rules, and Exercises on them, ... 10

SECTION III.
    Difficult Dissyllables, and Exercises on them, . . . 13

SECTION IV.
    Words sounded alike, but spelled differently, and Exercises on them, ... 16

SECTION V.
    Words not sounded alike, but apt to be confounded in spelling, with Exercises on them, ... 24
    Exercises on Possessive Case, ... 28
    Cautions, ... 29

SECTION VI.
    Alphabetical List of Difficult Polysyllables, . . . 29

SECTION VII.
    Etymology—Prefixes—Affixes—Roots—Compound Roots, with numerous Exercises, ... 34

SECOND PART.

MISCELLANEOUS DICTATION EXERCISES, ...	60
EXTRACTS FROM NEWSPAPERS, ...	106
FORMS OF LETTERS, ...	116
WORDS MIS-SPELT BY CANDIDATES FOR THE CIVIL SERVICE,	123
LATIN AND FRENCH PHRASES IN COMMON USE, . . .	127

Digitized by the Internet Archive
in 2007 with funding from
Microsoft Corporation

http://www.archive.org/details/spellingdictatio00edinrich

EXERCISES IN
SPELLING, DICTATION, AND ETYMOLOGY.

FIRST PART.

Section I.—LISTS OF THE MOST DIFFICULT MONOSYLLABLES IN COMMON USE.[1]

List I.

where	thief	wield	one
there	chief	shield	once
their	brief	shriek	some
vein	grief	siege	come
veil	fierce	seize	none
rein	pierce	niece	whose
prey	field	piece	eye
pour	said	blue	talk
four	whole	glue	walk
soul	blew	work	chalk
mourn	flew	worm	could
mould	crew	world	would
court	drew	worse	should
source	brew	month	view

[1] Except where there is a manifest advantage in inserting them, those words are here omitted which come more aptly in another connexion. The biliteral substitutes for the vowels (*e.g.*, *ai* for *a*, *ea* for *e*, *oa* for *o*, &c.,) do not involve any difficulty.

SPELLING AND DICTATION.

health	spread	learn	wasp
wealth	breath	pear	wash
lead	breast	wear	wound
head	meant	tear	youth
read	earth	break	soup
bread	deaf	great	group
thread	death	was	tour

touch	juice	bruise	strength
young	sluice	cruise	scheme
scourge	guide	guess	calm
buy	guile	guest	alms
build	guilt	give	choir
suit	bunch	learn	chasm
fruit	lunch	scene	shone
deign	friend	scythe	chord
feign	half	quoit	wharf
rhyme	halve	thyme	shoe

Dictation Exercises on List I.

(1.) I have read that there have been some men of such great courage, that they have been ready to bear the scourge, to endure wounds and bruises, and even to yield eir last breath, and to face death, in behalf of their tive country.

(2.) I told a group of four or five idle young men, who stood talking together, not to touch the soup which had been prepared for the poor, to avoid the guilt which would attach to their doing so, and if they wished for lunch to buy for themselves a bunch of grapes or some other fruit, or, if this did not suit their tastes, to eat of the bread which was spread out before them in plenty at their own homes.

(3.) Once on a time, as I walked in the city, I saw four thieves come to grief, and mourn in a court of justice the idleness of their youth, which had been the source of all their misery.

(4.) One day I saw an eagle, whose eye seemed to pierce the air, rise with a loud shriek from a rock, and seize a young hare which sat on the earth in a field about a mile off. He then flew up into the blue sky with outspread wings, to the place where his nest was built, and there began to tear his prey to pieces.

(5.) I could guess neither the name of my guest, nor that of his heir, who was with him, though the former had been my best friend at school, where we had planned together many a scheme of pleasure, nor would he deign to tell it me, but feigned not to see what I desired.

List II.—*Difficult Monosyllables continued.*

knee	debt	ought	wrong
kneel	✓vague	✓thought	wrench
✓ knife	vogue	bought	✓ wreck
know	✓ rogue	brought	write
✓ knock	✓ plague	✓wrought	wrote
✓knave	✓psalm	wrist	wren
doubt	✓ hymn	wrest	wry

wrap	sword	cough	sight
wrath	though	bough	bright
wharf	dough	plough	eighth
gnaw	through	nigh	weigh
gnash	rough	sigh	weight
gnat	tough	thigh	freight
tongue	trough	sign	height
league	chaise	sword	neigh
ache	skein	yacht	fraught
myrrh	niche	sour	taught

SPELLING AND DICTATION.

Dictation Exercises on List II.

(1.) Put away that knife, and kneel by me, while I tell you by what signs to know knaves and rogues when you meet them, though they may try to hide their wrong-doing, and to speak with a smooth tongue.

(2.) If you doubt whether you owe any man a debt, you ought to go and ask him. If you feel wrath against a friend, you should try to get rid of it before the night comes, lest it should be fraught with evil to your soul.

(3.) One day, under the shade of a spreading bough, he told me of his shipwreck: how the vessel weighed anchor and left the wharf on a cruise with a heavy freight, under the bright light of a morning sun: how she ploughed her way through a rough sea for many days: and how, on the eighth day, her tough planks began to give way, and the bolts to be wrenched out by the force of the hurricane: how the ship then rolled over into the trough of the sea, the waves rising to a great height on every side—a frightful sight—till at last the noble vessel went to pieces,—a few sailors only being brought safely to shore on its fragments, after tossing about all night.

Section II.—SPELLING RULES.

RULE I.—Final *y, preceded by a consonant,* becomes *i* when the word is increased in length.[1]

Examples.

try	pity	envy	glory
trial	pitiful	envious	glorious
tries	pities	envies	glories

[1] The contracted forms of the past participle prefer *t*, though preceded by a vowel; for example—

paid	*for*	payed		*Also* gaiety
laid		layed		daily
said		sayed		

Exceptions.

(1.) duteous   piteous   beauteous
    plenteous   bounteous
    dry   shy   sly
    dryness   shyness   slyness

(2.) The *y* is not changed before *ing*, because this would make an awkward word; nor in names of persons.

Examples.

fry   carry   marry
fry·ing   carry·ing   marry·ing
    Henry   Mary
    Henrys   Marys

Dictation Exercises on Rule I.

(1.) The chimneys in the houses of the mountain valleys send forth a beautiful vapour.

(2.) Busier no man could be than William, happier none; merrier or lovelier daughters than his I could have defied you to find; a tidier wife, and one displaying readier hospitality, or a more plentiful board, you could not have met with.

(3.) Write the third person, singular number, of the verbs buy, tarry, pity, obey, marry, reply.

Write the plural number of lily, valley, alley, ally, daisy, monkey.

Write the adjectives from study, duty, plenty.

Add *ness* to sly, shy, dry.

RULE II.—Words ending with a *single* consonant, if preceded by *only one vowel*, usually double the consonant when they are increased in length by the addition of another syllable.

Examples.

wet   fulfil   run
wetter   fulfilling   running

Exceptions.

Most words not accented on the last syllable and not ending in *l*.

Examples.

benefit	offer	ballot	visit
benefiting	offering	balloting	visitor

Dictation Exercises on Rule II.

(1.) The vessel was floating on the surface of the water.

(2.) The traveller was counselled to be quiet, and told that if he did not willingly obey he would be compelled to do so.

(3.) We visited the town and allotted the shares; some appealed, but their appeals were repelled when they were beginning to state them.

(4.) I never conferred with a sadder or a lazier man, and I limited my requests to a very few things.

(5.) Add *ed* or *ing* to hug, infer, shelter, pocket, wait, begin, rival, beg, sob, revel, dispel, inherit, drop, droop, equal, prefer, shudder, stab, cut, wrap, repeal, omit defer, differ, regret, suffer.

RULE III.—Where an affix *beginning with a vowel* (such as *able, ible, al, ous, ant, y*) is added to a word ending with the vowel *e*, the *e* is dropt.

Examples.

remove	live	nature
removal	living	natural
force	please	blame
forcible	pleasant	blamable

Exceptions.

(1.) The *e* is retained when the dropping of it would cause confusion or difficulty.

Examples.

agree	dye	hoe	shoe	singe
agreeable	dyeing	hoeing	shoeing	singeing

(2.) The *e* before *able* or *ous* is retained when it is preceded by *c* or *g* soft.

Examples.

change	notice	outrage
changeable	noticeable	outrageous
advantage		courage
advantageous		courageous

Peculiarities.

die	lie	tie
dying	lying	tying

Exercises on Rule III.

(1.) Add *al, ible, able, ing,* or *ous* to blame, brute, bribe, tame, civilize, engage, purchase, grieve, excuse, mistake, consume, imagine.

(2.) He may be both famous and agreeable, and in many respects truly admirable, but his recent conduct is neither excusable in itself, nor reconcilable with his character.

(3.) He was able to tame the unmanageable beast, but with the greatest difficulty conceivable ; and it would not be advisable for any one to imitate his example.

(4.) I found the traveller lying on his bed apparently in a dying condition. Lest my conduct should be considered blamable, I directed his removal to a more agreeable residence where he might be benefited by purer air and by cheerful visitors. There was soon a noticeable improvement in his health.

Section III.—DIFFICULT DISSYLLABLES IN COMMON USE.[1]

abyss	adieu	ancient	assign
access	adjourn	answer	assuage
accrue	aggrieve	antique	asthma
achieve	aghast	anxious	autumn
acre	ague	arraign	awkward
address	almond	askew	bargain

---

[1] The spelling of which cannot be easily ascertained either from the sound of the words or by applying the spelling rules.

SPELLING AND DICTATION.

bazaar	besiege	busy	career
beautify	biscuit	breakfast	carriage
beguile	blaspheme	canoe	cashier
belief	borough	campaign	centre
believe	bosom	caprice	chagrin
benign	burgher	captain	chamois

champagne	cocoa	conceive	contour
chasten	coerce	condemn	country
chemist	colour	conduit	couple
chieftain	column	construe	cousin
chorus	colleague	contemn	creature
christen	conceit	contempt	crescent
circuit			

crevice	cynic	disguise	empty
crystal	cypher	docile	endue
cuirass	cypress	double	enough
cupboard	daughter	doughty	epoch
cushion	deceive	echo	eschew
cycle	diphthong	eclipse	exhaust

falcon	gesture	guitar	hyssop
famine	ghastly	halfpence	impugn
fatigue	grandeur	harangue	indict
feudal	gristle	heifer	intrigue
flourish	grotesque	heinous	inveigh
foreign	guinea	hostler	island

issue	leather	luncheon	measles
knowledge	leisure	lyric	minute
knuckle	leopard	machine	mischief
labour	lettuce	malign	missile
language	linguist	marine	money
languor	liquor	meadow	mortgage

SPELLING AND DICTATION. 15

muscle	nuisance	people	pleasure
mystic	oblique	perceive	poignant
neighbour	ocean	persuade	poniard
nephew	opaque	pheasant	poultry
neuter	pageant	physic	precede
nourish	peasant	pigeon	proceed
profile	receive	rhubarb	sceptic
prorogue	recruit	roguish	sceptre
quadrille	reprieve	routine	schedule
qualmish	resign	salmon	scissors
quarrel	resume	sanguine	seamstress
recede	retrieve	saucer	sergeant
shepherd	soldier	sulphur	thorough
shoulder	solemn	surfeit	tissue
shovel	spectre	surgeon	tortoise
sinew	subtle	syntax	treasure
slaughter	succeed	syringe	uncouth
sojourn.	sugar	thistle	unique
	victuals	wainscot	wrestle
	villain	weapon	yeoman
	viscount	whistle	zealous

Dictation Exercises on difficult Dissyllables.

(1.) The condemned captive did not perceive fully the mischief he had done in the course of his busy but wicked career, and to the last moment he anxiously looked for a reprieve, and could not be brought to believe that he was deceiving himself with vain hopes. The ghastly look of mingled horror and chagrin which was visible in his face when he was at last compelled to ascend the carriage sent to convey him to that solemn death to which he could not resign himself, was a piteous sight.

(2.) The chorus of the birds in the early spring, when they never seem to know fatigue in the busy work of building their nests, the glory of the bright summer, and the beautiful colours of the autumn, are all signs of the benign nature of Him who made all things, and sustains them by his power.

(3.) We found victuals of all sorts in the bazaar of the ancient island city—bread, biscuits, and liquor, and made some thoroughly good bargains, which retrieved the losses incurred during the winter campaign.

(4.) As we proceeded on our way over the pleasant meadow, under the light of the crescent moon, he told me how he had succeeded in making so much money. From a peasant he had become a soldier, at the desire of a recruiting sergeant; he soon became weary of the routine of his life, and assuming a disguise, and disregarding the warnings of his conscience, had almost escaped into a foreign country, when he was taken and severely punished. He then crossed the ocean with his comrades to fight the battles of his country, till exhausted by the climate and his wounds, he was discharged, and with nothing but his knapsack on his shoulder, found his way to a colony. There the knowledge he had gained became useful, and he flourished as well as the most sanguine could have wished. As I heard him rehearse the story of his life, I felt persuaded that the colonies were the best spheres of labour for the sturdy yeoman as well as for the scantily nourished peasant.

Section IV.—WORDS SOUNDED ALIKE BUT SPELLED DIFFERENTLY.

He gave all he had.
The awl of a shoemaker.

Ere (before) he arrived.
The heir of an estate.
The air we breathe.

Has he aught in his hand?
Ought we to do it?

The busy little ant.
My aunt Jane.

The apples he ate.
Twice four are eight.

A bale of goods.
He was bail for his friend.

SPELLING AND DICTATION.   17

A round ball.
A loud bawl.
His legs were bare.
A savage bear.
A base fellow.
A bass voice.

We drink beer.
We carry the dead on a bier.
A ripe berry.
Bury the dead.
The birth of a child.
A berth in a ship.

A brake of brushwood.
To break a stick.
Bred up to be a sailor.
A loaf of bread.
To stand by a chair.
To buy a new hat.

To cite before a magistrate.
The site of a house.
The eyesight.
A sultry clime (for climate).
To climb a hill.
Close the door.
Put on your clothes.

A narrow creek or bay.
The gate will creak.
The deer in the park.
A dear child.

A beech tree.
The sea-beach.
He had been there before.
A garden bean.
To be a man.
A honey-bee.

The wind blew.
A blue dress.
To bore a hole.
A wild boar.
The bough of a tree.
To bow the head.

A hole is bored through a board.
The ceiling of a room.
Sealing-wax.
It hung by a cord.
The chord of a harp.

The choler of an angry man.
His collar was clean.
A coarse thread.
A man's course in life.
The core of an apple.
A corps of volunteers.

The sick man will die.
To dye a dress.
A draft on a bank.
A draught of water.
The draught of a plan.

B

The morning dew.
The bill is due (owing).

My feet are bare.
The feat of a brave soldier.

To flee from a foe.
A flea bites.

Railway fare.
A fair face.
A fair price.

The bird flew away.
The flue of a stove.

The fore foot of a horse.
A horse has four feet.

The army went forth.
The fourth boy in the class.

Foul water.
A fowl lays eggs.

Furs of animals.
Furze blossoms are yellow.

The gate of the farmyard.
An awkward gait in walking.

A gilt picture frame.
The guilt of lying.

A sorrowful groan.
The boy has grown fast.

The fire grate.
To grate to powder.
A great man.

A hale (healthy) man.
A storm of hail.

The hall of a house.
To haul in a net.

A hart—a stag.
A man's heart.

The heel of the foot.
To heal a disease.

Come here to me.
Hear what I say.

A swift hare.
A boy with red hair.

A herd of cattle.
He heard a voice.

Hew down a tree.
A bright hue (colour).

Let us go and see him.
We sang a hymn.

A horde of savages.
A miser's hoard.

I will go now.
Open your eye.

The isle or island.
The aisle of a church.

He went in a cab.
He went to an inn.

SPELLING AND DICTATION.

The door-key.
Ship anchored at the quay.
To kill a man.
A brick-kiln.
The horse was led.
A lead mine.

To levy recruits.
To attend a levée.
A lone (or lonely) house.
The loan of a book.
The tailor made a coat.
The maid-servant.

A male animal.
A mail-coach.
The mane of a horse.
A main street.
The mantel-piece of a room.
A woman's mantle.

A field-marshal in the army.
A martial (warlike) nation.
A mean fellow.
The mien of a gentleman.
The meed of valour.
A grass mead or meadow.

We meet a friend.
We eat meat.
Mete or measure out justice.
A gas-meter.
Metre or measure of a verse.
Mity cheese.
A mighty (powerful) man.

A moan of grief.
The grass is mown.
We say nay for no.
The neigh of a horse.
We need food daily.
The baker must knead bread.

A new book.
We knew he would come.
A stormy night.
A brave knight in armour.
We will not go.
Tie the string in a knot.

No, it cannot be done.
Do you know your lesson?
My nose is cold.
He knows how to ride.
Gold and silver ore.
We row a boat with an oar.

A pale face.
The garden pale.
A pail of water.
Our kind friends.
We go in an hour.
A pane of glass.
A pain in the head.

Pare me an apple.
A pair of shoes.
A nice ripe pear.
A pause in reading.
The lion's paws.
A time of peace.
A piece of cake.

SPELLING AND DICTATION.

Orange-peel.
A peal of bells.
A carpenter's plane.
A wide grassy plain.
The pores of the skin.
He pours out the beer.
John pores over his book.

A long wooden pole.
The poll of the head.
We pray for pardon.
A beast of prey.
It is going to rain.
The reign of a king.
Lead the horse by the rein.

The rays of the sun.
Raze a house to the ground.
Stare at a strange sight.
The house stair.
A stationer sells stationery.
China is stationary.

A steel knife.
A thief will steal.
A stile into the field.
A good style of writing.
A narrow strait.
A straight line.

A sum of money.
Some plum-cake.
The sun shines.
My uncle's little son.
Tacks for the carpet.
The window tax.

I read a pretty tale.
The cow's tail.
The valleys teem with corn.
A team of horses.
The time of day.
A plant of thyme.

We met the man there.
Give them their pens.

Tom threw the ball.
We went through a lane.

The queen's throne.
The rider was thrown.

Too many men went up.
John asked to go too.
Twice one are two.
The toe of the foot.
Tow is made from flax.
A tea tray.
A trait in his character.

A treatise on government.
Treaties between nations.

A vane on a steeple.
A vain child.
A vein in the arm.

A fertile vale.
A woman's veil.

A waste piece of ground.
The waist of the body.

Wait for me.
Carry a heavy weight.

The merchant sells his ware.
I wear my hat.

SPELLING AND DICTATION. 21

A long way to London.
Weigh the sugar.
Fine weather.
A wether sheep.
He stayed a week.
His uncle was a weak man.

Rap at a door.
Wrap yourself up.
Reeds grow by the water.
Read your book.
A red rose.
John read the letter.

We rest from work.
Wrest off the bell-handle.
Frost covers with rime.
Can you write rhyme?
A diamond ring.
Wring the neck of a fowl.

A religious rite.
We will do what is right.
Write a letter.
Fetch a wheelwright.
He rode on horseback.
The road was dry.

The roe of a fish.
A row of peas.
Learn by rote.
He wrote to his mother.
A field of rye.
A wry neck.

A sale by auction.
The sail of a ship.
We sow seed.
We cede (give up) our claim.
A bishop's see.
I see with my eyes.
Ships sail on the sea.

A horse was seen in the field.
We beheld a fair scene.
Sell me a loaf.
A prisoner's cell.
The boy was sent home.
Roses have a sweet scent.

A large or small size.
She weeps and sighs.
The skull of the head.
A small boat is a scull.
A slight thread.
Sleight of hand.

A slow coach.
A wild sloe.
He thinks so.
The farmer sows seed.
Jane sews her dress.

A sore place.
The eagles soar in the air.
The sole of the foot.
The sole (only) reason.
A man's immortal soul.

A stake of wood.
A beef-steak.
Our side won the game.
One man was left.
A thick wood.
He would go on.

A weak man.
Seven days make a week.
A heavy yoke.
The yolk of an egg.
You may go.
A large yew-tree.
The ewe lost her lamb.

DICTATION EXERCISES ON WORDS SOUNDED ALIKE, BUT SPELLED DIFFERENTLY.

(1.) The hare leaped over a gate, and the boy began to climb a stile close by, but the bough of a beech-tree caught his clothes, tearing more than one large hole in them. He fell in the road over a piece of wood, but soon sprang to his feet, and though he had lost the sole off his old pair of boots, he kept steadily on his course.

The little four-footed beast, swift as a deer, rushed into a great wood, and then across a mead where a herd of cattle was feeding near some reeds. When the boy came to this spot he made a mighty effort to kill the hare, but it escaped again, led him on into a brake of furze, and as it would not come forth, he left it there, and went his way.

The air was fresh; all the trees were in leaf; the ants and bees were busy; a bean-field near was in blossom. He found a berry of a blue colour, called a sloe, and as he had some bread and beer or ale in his pocket, he ate them together, and made a good dinner.

While eating, he sat on a low bank covered with coarse grass and thyme; the bright sky was his ceiling; the sun had dried up the dew, and its rays fell on plain, and vale, and hill. A horse close by began to neigh, and toss his mane and tail, while he galloped over the plain. A red rose of the deepest dye grew at his right hand, and gave out a sweet scent; a thistle-seed floated by. Afar off he saw the sea and a sail on it; a gull soared aloft, and he watched it till his eyes closed, and he took a long nap.

After a time he woke, and felt lone and strange. The sun was low, and the night was coming on. A yew-tree near looked black; the weather was changing; some rain fell. He did not wait a moment, but ran straight home through the wood and across the waste field where he had been thrown down in the morning. He reached the house too late for tea; but hungry enough to enjoy such coarse fare as could be had.

(2.) The culprit stole a bale of goods,
Which landed him in jail;
He then gave up the bale of goods,
And for himself gave bail.

(3.) If a brother offend in aught, we ought, if he be penitent, to forgive him freely; for thus saith the Scripture: "If thy brother trespass against thee, rebuke him; and if he repent, forgive him." A great poet says—
"To err is human, to forgive divine."

(4.) The bell in the tower sounds clear;
A belle with gay colours is dight;
The former appeals to the ear,
The latter appeals to the sight.

(5.) He that is duly bred to labour, will find labour bread to him.

(6.) From dough we get bread, from doe we get meat;
Very fair fare for the hungry to eat.

(7.) Every dog has four legs; but no dog has his fore legs behind.

(8.) I need bread, and you knead bread; and yet I am in want of bread, and you are not.

(9.) 'Tis surely meet that we should mete
Each man his meat when due,
Lest we should meet, what would be meet,
Delay and hunger too.

(10.) His spirit in his mien we see,
For surely a spirit mean has he.

SPELLING AND DICTATION.

Section V.—WORDS NOT SOUNDED ALIKE, BUT APT TO BE CONFOUNDED IN SPELLING.

Accept, to take or receive.
Except, to leave out.
Affect, to move the feelings.
Effect, to bring about.
Accidents, chances.
Accidence, elements of grammar.

Aunt, a parent's sister.
Ant, an insect.
Adherence, clinging to.
Adherents, those who cling to.
Acts, deeds.
Axe, tool for chopping

Assistants, helpers.
Assistance, help.
Addition, something added.
Edition, a publication.
Arrant, notorious.
Errant, wandering.
Errand, a message.

Accede, to agree to.
Exceed, to go beyond.
Alley, a passage.
Ally, a friend and helper.
Aloud, audibly.
Allowed, permitted.

Altar, a place for an offering.
Alter, to change.
Bridal, relating to a marriage.
Bridle, a rein.
Broach, to make a hole in a cask.
Brooch, an ornament.

Bald, hairless.
Bawled, called aloud.
Board, a plank.
Bored, did bore.
Britain, name of a country.
Briton, an inhabitant of Britain.

Celery, a vegetable.
Salary, wages.
Complaisant, polite.
Complacent, pleased with one's-self.
Confidant, one trusted with secrets.
Confident, self-assured.

Currant, a small dried grape.
Current, a stream.
Counsel, advice or to advise.
Council, a deliberative assembly.
Concert, a musical performance.
Consort, a companion.

SPELLING AND DICTATION.

Correspondents, those who correspond.
Correspondence, letters interchanged; agreement.
Censure, blame.
Censor, one who blames.
Censer, a vessel for holding incense.

Cellar, an underground room.
Seller, one who sells.
Cease, to stop.
Seize, to lay hold of.
Calendar, a book of dates.
Calender, a press to smooth linen.

Dire, dreadful.
Dyer, one who dyes.
Deference, respect.
Difference, disagreement.
Decent, becoming.
Descent, a going down.
Dissent, to differ from.

Disease, an ailment.
Decease, death.
Desert, to forsake.
Dessert, fruit after dinner.
Extant, existent.
Extent, space.

Elicit, to draw out.
Illicit, unlawful.

Elude, to escape from.
Illude, to deceive.

Eminent, noted.
Imminent, dangerous.

Eruption, a breaking out.
Irruption, a breaking into.
Emigrant, one leaving his home to reside in another country.
Immigrant, one having come to reside in another country.
Envelop, to cover.
Envelope, a cover.

Fisher, one who fishes.
Fissure, a rent.
Flour, ground grain.
Flower, the blossom of a plant.
Fir, a tree.
Fur, the hairy covering of an animal.

Genius, mental gifts.
Genus, a kind.
Goal, a starting-point.
Gaol, a prison.
Gamble, to play a game of chance.
Gambol, to play.

Hoarse, rough-voiced.
Horse, an animal.
Holy, religious.
Wholly, entirely.
Ingenious, clever.
Ingenuous, open, candid.

Impostor, one who deceives
Imposture, deception.
Idle, not doing anything.
Idol, an image.
Instants, moments.
Instance, example.

Least, smallest.
Lest, for fear.
Lessen, to make less.
Lesson, a school task.
Lair, the couch of a wild beast.
Layer, one who lays; something laid down.

Lose, to mislay.
Loose, not tight.
Liniment, ointment.
Lineament, a feature.
Legislator, a law-maker.
Legislature, the assembly which makes laws.

Medal, a coin.
Meddle, to interfere.
Morning, the early part of the day.
Mourning, clothes worn for the dead.
Mare, a female horse.
Mayor, a chief magistrate.

Metal, a kind of mineral.
Mettle, spirit, courage.
Manner, way of doing anything.
Manor, an estate.
Missed, did miss.
Mist, fog.

Monetary, belonging to money.
Monitory, warning.
Opposite, contrary.
Apposite, well-suited.
Ordinance, a decree.
Ordnance, cannon.

Principal, chief.
Principle, original cause, or a rule.
Palate, the roof of the mouth.
Pallet, a little bed.
Plaintiff, one who complains.
Plaintive, complaining.

SPELLING AND DICTATION.

Prophecy, a foretelling.
Prophesy, to foretell.

Prophet, one who foretells.
Profit, gain.

Pearl, a precious stone.
Peril, danger.

Patience, forbearance.
Patients, sick people.

Presence, being in view.
Presents, gifts.

Pastor, a shepherd, hence a clergyman.
Pasture, feeding-ground.

Preposition, a part of speech.
Proposition, a sentence.
Regimen, a rule.
Regiment, a number of soldiers.
Shone, the past tense of shine.
Shown, the past tense of show.

Scroll, a roll of papers.
Scrawl, bad writing.
Symbol, a sign.
Cymbal, a musical instrument.
Sects, parties.
Sex, kind (male or female).

Sculptor, a carver of stone.
Sculpture, carved stone figures.
Species, a kind.
Specious, showy.
Statue, an image.
Statute, a law.
Stature, height of a person.

Talents, gifts of mind.
Talons, claws of birds.
Track, a path.
Tract, a short treatise.
Weather, state of atmosphere.
Whether, which of two.

Wreak, to exercise vengeance.
Wreck, destruction.
Whales, marine animals.
Wales, a portion of Great Britain.

Weal, prosperity.
Wheel, part of a carriage.
Whither, to what place.
Wither, to waste away.

---

* N.B.—The pupil should be exercised on the above by being required to construct sentences containing a few of the words apt to be confounded.

DICTATION EXERCISES ON WORDS APT TO BE CONFOUNDED, THOUGH NOT SOUNDED ALIKE.

[Write the words apt to be confounded with those to which an asterisk is appended, giving the meaning of each.]

(1.) The merchant, who was more complacent* than complaisant* in his manner, affected* not to accept* the salary* which was allowed,* although in reality he retained the principal* part of it.

(2.) The immigrant* knew* not whither* to bend his course,* but he had so little deference* for the counsel* of others, and was so confident* of his own talents,* that in the morning* he mounted his horse,* and, with no weapon except* an axe,* he rode* into the desert* heedless of the imminent* peril* to which he exposed himself, and wholly* ignorant of the goal* towards which he should direct his steps.

(3.) The idle* and impudent* impostor,* having been sent on an errand* into the forest, said that he could find the track* without the least* assistance.*

(4.) You may dissent* from me, but ingenious* as you are, you cannot elude* the proposition* I have made, or alter* the statute* which ought to guide your conduct,— the ordinance* which the legislature* has passed.

(5.) As he left the concert,* he tried to envelop* himself in a species* of cloak, which consisted of two blankets sewed* together, lined with fur,* and fastened in front with a brooch.*

Exercise on Possessive Case.

The agents' warehouses contained our father's property hich he had bequeathed to his sons' sons and his daughters' daughters. But we could at first get no information when the ship came to port. When her arrival was known, the captain's wife and his brother's four daughters went on board. They were greeted by the sailors' cheers; one man's enthusiasm being so great that he threw his brother's cap overboard. The men's manners were better than their clothes. The captain's wife was touched by their greeting, and the young ladies' eyes were filled with tears. We had to wait patiently.

CAUTIONS.
Prefixes apt to be confounded in Spelling.

ante (Latin), *before*: antedate, antecedent.
anti (Greek), *against*: antipathy, antidote.
de, down: descent, defer, deprive, decease.
dis, di, asunder or *apart*: dissent, disjoin, disease, differ, divert.

The prefixes *mis* and *dis* often lead to misspelling, because the writer does not observe whether the words with which they are conjoined begin with an *s* or not; for example, *mistake, misspell, misstate, dissatisfaction, disorder.*

A similar mistake is apt to happen with other prefixes, especially *in* and *con;* for example, innocuous, inefficient. The pupil has simply to notice whether the principal part of the word begins with the same letter that the prefix ends with. In that case the letter is doubled.[1]

Section VI.—ALPHABETICAL LIST OF DIFFICULT POLYSYLLABLES IN COMMON USE.

abeyance	accessary	accompany
academy	accession	accomplice
accelerate	accommodation	accoutrement ✓

[1] Those who do not know Latin can learn when to use *en* or *in* at the beginning, and *able, ible, ant, ance, ent, ence, er, or, our* at the end of words, only from practice. So with many other words to which the Latin (and frequently the Greek) is the only sure guide.

accumulate
acknowledge
acquiesce
acquisition
adequate
adulterate
advertisement
aërial
aëronaut
agreeable
algebraical
allegiance
allusive
alluvial
almanac
amiable
amphibious
analogy
ancestor
annihilation
anniversary
anomaly
anonymous
antecedent
antediluvian
antipodes
anxiety
apology
apostasy
apostrophe
appetite
appreciate
aqueduct
aqueous
archangel
architect

arithmetician
artifice
ascendant
ascendency
ascertain
ascetic
assiduous
assimilate
association
astronomical
asthmatic
attorney
atrocious
audacity
auxiliary

barricade
battalion
bayonet
belligerent
beneficially
business

capitulate
catalogue
catastrophe
catechism
cathedral
celebrate
celerity
ceremony
ceremonious
certificate
chalybeate

chameleon
characteristically
chimerical
christianity
chronological
circumstance
circumstantial
coalesce
cognizance
coincidence
colloquial
colloquy
colonnade
colossal
commemorate
commiserate
committee
companion
compensate
complacent
conciliatory
concurrence
condescend
confederate
connoisseur
conqueror
consanguinity
conscientious
consummate
contiguous
contrariety
contumely
contumelious
convalescence
co-operation
coquetry

SPELLING AND DICTATION. 31

correspondence	dishonourable	epitaph
corroborate	dissatisfaction ✓	equestrian
councillor	dissimilar	equipage
counsellor	dissuasive	✓ equivalent
counteract	✓ dissyllable	erroneous
counterfeit	domestic	escutcheon
✓ courageous	dubiety	especial
courteous	dynasty	ethereal
criticism		etiquette
		etymology
	eccentric	eulogium
✓ decalogue	ecclesiastical	evanescent
decipher	effeminate	evangelical
decisive	effervesce	exaggerate
deficiency	✓ efficacy	✓ exchequer
degenerate	egregious	excogitate
✓ deleterious	electricity	excrescence
deliberative	eligible	execrable
delicacy	emaciate	exhibit
delineate	emancipate	✓ exhilarate
✓ delirious	emergency	expatiate
demagogue	emetic	explicit
demeanour	emphasis	exquisite
depreciate	emphatic	extempore
deteriorate	enamour	extraordinary
develop	encouragement	extravagance
dialogue	✓ encyclopædia	
dilemma	endeavour	
✓ diocese	endorsement	✓ facetious
diocesan	energetic	feasible
disappointment	enfranchise	felicitous
discernible	enlargement	functionary
disciple	enrolment	
discipline	enthralment	
discourage	envelop	✓ gazetteer
✓ dishevel	episcopacy	genealogy

generally
generosity
geographical
geography
gorgeous
government
guarantee
gymnastic

halcyon
hemisphere
homicide
honorary
hydraulics
hypocrisy
hypocrite
hypothesis
hysterics

illegible
illusion
imbecile
impossible
inaccessible
incendiary
incessantly
incipient
incorporeal
incorrigible
indefatigable
indefinite
indelible
indissoluble
indivisibility

inefficacious
inexorable
ingratiate
initiate
iniquitous
inscrutable
instalment
insufficiency
intelligible
interruption
interstice
inveigle
irascible
irrelevant
irreproachable
irretrievable

jealousy
jeopardy
judicious

legislator
legislature
licentiate
lieutenant
lineament
liniment
longevity
lugubrious

machination
machinery
magisterial

magnificently
mahogany
maintenance
manœuvre
marauder
martyrdom
masquerade
massacre
mathematician
mechanic
mechanism
medicinal
medicine
melancholy
metaphorical
metaphysical
microscope
miniature
miscellaneous
miscellany
mischievous
misdemeanour
monastery
monopoly
municipal
munificent
myriad
mystery
mythology

nauseous
necessarily
necessitate
negotiate
notoriety

SPELLING AND DICTATION.

obediently
obeisance
obloquy
obsequious
omniscient
omnivorous
outrageously

panegyrist
parallel
paralleled
parallelogram
paralytic
parliamentary
parochial
patriarch
perusal
philosophical
phlegmatic
phraseology
physician
physiognomy
picturesque
plebeian
political
pomegranate
porcelain
portmanteau
possession
poulterer
precipice
precocious
predecessor
prescience
primeval

principality
privilege
proficiency
prophetic
proselyte
protuberance
pusillanimity
putrefaction
putrefy
pyramid

quiescent
quintessence

raillery
reciprocal
reconcile
rehearsal
reiterate
remediable
reminiscence
rendezvous
repartee
reservoir
retinue
reverberate
rhapsody
rhetoric
rheumatism

sacrilege
sagacious
satellite
satiety

schismatic
scholastic
scientific
sententious
separate
septennial
sepulchre
sequestrate
seraphic
seraglio
simultaneous
sinecure
society
solicitude
soliloquy
sovereign
specimen
spontaneous
stomachic
subaltern
subterranean
successively
superannuated
supercilious
supernumerary
surreptitious
susceptible
sycamore
syllogism
synonymous
synopsis
systematical

telescope
terrestrial

c

topographical   ubiquity   vicinity
tournament   unanimous   vicissitude
tragedian   vociferous
tranquillity
transcendent   vehemently
typographical   ventriloquism   zoology
tyrannically   vestibule   zoological

Section VII.—ETYMOLOGY.

N.B.—*Roots and their derivatives have properly no place in a book, the object of which is to teach spelling; but prefixes and affixes have so very important a bearing on the spelling of words, and so frequently serve as a guide to the writer, that we have ventured to introduce here very ample exercises on them. These exercises will be found extremely valuable in other respects.*[1]

EXPLANATION OF THE PREFIXES.

Each prefix in this section is defined, and then illustrated by an example. The prefixes, with their definitions, should be thoroughly committed to memory. In reciting the examples, the pupils should *pronounce* and *spell* the word, before giving the definition.

Exercise 1.

Prefixes.	Force.	Examples.	Definitions.
AB	*from; away.*	AB SOLVE',	to free *from.*
AD	*to; at; near.*	AD JOIN',	to join *to.*
ANA	*up; again.*	AN' A LYSE,	to loosen *up;* resolve
ANTE	*before.*	AN TE CED' ENT,	going *before.*
ANTI	*against; opposite.*	AN TIP' A THY,	feeling *against;* ill-will.
BE	*by; over.*	BE SIDE',	*by* or *near* the side
BENE	*well.*	BEN E FAC' TOR,	one who does *well.*
CIRCUM	*around; about.*	CIR CUM' FLUENT,	flowing *around.*
CIS	*on this side.*	CIS AT LAN' TIC,	*this side* the Atlantic

[1] The compiler is indebted for the excellent arrangement of the lessons on prefixes and affixes to an American spelling-book.

SPELLING AND DICTATION. 35

Prefixes.	Force.	Examples.	Definitions.
Con	*with; together.*	Con voke′,	to call *together.*
Contra	*against.*	Con tra dict′,	to speak *against.*

Exercise 2.

De	*from; down.*	De part′,	to part *from.*
Dis	*apart; away.*	Dis miss′,	to send *away.*
E	*out; out of; from.*	E ject′,	to cast *out.*
En	*in; to make or put.*	En wrap′.	to wrap *in.*
Extra	*beyond.*	Ex tra mun′ dane,	*beyond* the world.
Fore	*before.*	Fore tell′,	to tell *beforehand.*
Hemi	*half.*	Hem′ i sphere,	a half *sphere.*
In	*in; into; not.*	In cise′,	to cut *in* or *into.*
Inter	*between; among.*	In ter pose′,	to put *between.*
Intro	*within; inward.*	In tro duce′,	to bring or lead *within.*
Mis	*wrong; bad.*	Mis guide′,	to guide *wrong.*
Male	*badly.*	Mal e fac′ tor,	one who does *badly.*

Exercise 3.

Ob	*in front; against.*	Ob ject′,	to throw or urge *against.*
Out	*beyond.*	Out run′,	to run *beyond;* outstrip.
Over	*above; beyond.*	O ver shoot′,	to shoot *beyond.*
Per	*through.*	Per′ fo rate,	to bore *through.*
Post	*after; afterwards.*	Post′ script,	what is written *after.*
Pre	*before.*	Pre judge′,	to judge *beforehand.*
Preter	*beyond; past.*	Pre ter nat′ u ral,	*beyond* nature.
Pro	*forth.*	Pro duce′,	to lead or bring *forth.*
Re	*again; back.*	Re view′,	to view *again.*
Retro	*backwards.*	Ret′ ro grade,	to go *backwards.*
Se	*aside; apart.*	Se cede′,	to go aside or apart.
Semi	*half.*	Sem′ i cir cle,	*half* a circle.

Exercise 4.

Sub	*under; after.*	Sub scribe′,	to write *under.*
Subter	*under.*	Sub ter ran′ e an,	*under* the earth.
Super	*over; above.*	Su per nat′ u ral,	*above* the natural
Syn	*with; together.*	Syn′ the sis,	a putting *together*
Sus[1]	*from under; up.*	Sus tain′,	to hold *up.*

---
[1] From *sub,* through the French *sous.*

Prefixes.	Force.	Examples.	Definitions.
TRANS	*across; over.*	TRAN SCEND',	to climb or pass *over.*
UP	*above; on high.*	UP LIFT',	to lift on *high.*
ULTRA	*beyond.*	UL TRA MON' TANE,	*beyond* the mountains.
UN	*not.*	UN HAP' PY,	*not* happy.
WITH	*against; away.*	WITH STAND',	to stand *against.*

REMARKS ON SOME OF THE PREFIXES.
Exercise 5.

Some of the prefixes have a variety of forms. This grows out of a regard to euphony; that is, a desire to produce agreeable sound. Thus, when AD (to) comes before a root or radical beginning with a consonant, the *d* of the prefix is generally changed into whatever consonant the radical begins with. In this way, for example, AD undergoes no less than ten different changes: AD, AC, AP, AG, AL, AN, AP, AR, AS, AT, A. The following are examples of words, in which all the various forms of AD appear.

Thus, instead of	AD CEPT,	we say,	AC CEPT'.
,,	AD FIX,	,,	AF FIX'.
,,	AD GRIEVE,	,,	AG GRIEVE'.
,,	AD LOT,	,,	AL LOT'.
,,	AD NEX,	,,	AN NEX'.
,,	AD PEND,	,,	AP PEND'.
,,	AD RANGE,	,,	AR RANGE'.
,,	AD SUME,	,,	AS SUME'.
,,	AD TRACT,	,,	AT TRACT'.
,,	AD SCEND,	,,	A SCEND'.

Exercise 6.

The other prefixes which, like AD, have different forms, are—

AB,	sometimes written	ABS or A: as, *Ab*stract, *A*vert.
ANTI,	,,	ANT: as, *Ant*arctic.
CON,	,,	COG, COL, COM, COR, or CO: *Cog*nate.
CONTRA,	,,	COUNTER: as *Counter*act.
DIS,	,,	DIF or DI: as, *Dif*fident, *Di*vert.
E,	,,	EX, EC, or EF: *Ex*press, *Ec*centric.

SPELLING AND DICTATION. 37

E̲n̲, sometimes written E̲m̲ : *Em*balm.
I̲n̲, ,, I̲g̲, I̲l̲, I̲m̲, or I̲r̲ : as, *Ig*noble, *Il*legal.
O̲b̲, ,, O̲c̲, O̲f̲, or O̲p̲ : *Oc*cur, *Of*fer, *Op*pose.
S̲u̲b̲, ,, S̲u̲c̲, S̲u̲f̲, S̲u̲g̲, or S̲u̲p̲ : as *Suc*ceed.
S̲y̲n̲, ,, S̲y̲l̲, S̲y̲m̲ : as, *Syl*lable.

Exercise 7.

When a Prefix means *not*, it is said to be NEGATIVE; as, *dis*like, *not* to like; *un*able, *not* able.

When a Prefix means *to deprive of*, or *to take out of the state of*, it is said to be PRIVATIVE; as, *dis*arm, to to deprive *of* arms.

The prefixes most used, in a privative or negative sense, are D̲e̲, D̲i̲s̲, I̲n̲, and U̲n̲; as,

D̲e̲ THRONE', *to deprive of* a throne.
D̲e̲ RANGE', *to take out of the state of being* in order.
D̲i̲s̲ SIM' I LAR, *not* similar, unlike.
I̲n̲ EL' E GANT, *not* elegant.
U̲n̲ GRATE' FUL, *not* grateful.
U̲n̲ BIND', *to take out of the state of being* bound.

Sometimes a prefix adds nothing to the meaning of a radical. In such case, it is said to be merely EUPHONIC; as, U̲n̲ in *un*loose, which does not affect the sense of the word *loose*—loose and *un*loose meaning the same thing.

EXPLANATIONS OF THE AFFIXES.

Exercise 8.

Affixes.	Force.	Examples.	Definitions.
A̲t̲e̲[1]	*to make.*	TERM' IN ATE,	*to make* an end.
E̲n̲	*to make.*	SOFT' EN,	*to make* soft.

---

[1] A̲t̲e̲ and E̲n̲, in common with F̲y̲, I̲f̲y̲, and I̲z̲e̲, are defined above by the phrase "*to make;*" because they are commonly used to form verbs. This phrase, "*to make,*" is taken, as a definition, merely for the sake of convenience. In many cases, other definitions, as "*to cause,*" "*to put,*" etc., will be found more suitable.

Besides this use, however, A̲t̲e̲ and E̲n̲, to which may be added the affix E̲d̲, are employed to form participles and participial adjectives; and are then

SPELLING AND DICTATION.

Affixes.	Force.	Examples.	Definitions.
Fy	*to make.*	Am'pli fy,	*to make* ample.
Ize	*to make.*	Civ'il ize,	*to make* civil.
Ish	*to make.*	Pub'lish,	*to make* public.
Ar	*one who.*	Beg'gar,	*one who* begs.
Er	*one who.*	Pay'er,	*one who* pays.
Or	*one who.*	Act'or,	*one who* acts.

Exercise 9.

Ist	*one who.*	Art'ist,	*one who* is skilled in art.
Ner	*one who.*	Part'ner,	*one who* has or owns a part.
Ster	*one who.*	Team'ster,	*one who* drives a team.
Yer	*one who.*	Law'yer,	*one who* is versed in law.
San	*one who.*	Par'ti san,	*one who* sides with a party.
Zen	*one who.*	Cit'i zen,	*one who* dwells in a city.
Ess	*a female.*	Li'on ess,	*a female* of the lion tribe.
Ine	*a female.*	Her'o ine,	a heroic woman.

Exercise 10.

Ity[1]	}		Pub lic'ity,	*quality or state of being* public.
Cy			Pri'vacy,	*quality or state of being* private.
Ance		*quality,*	Vig'il ance,	*state of being* vigilant.
Ency	}	*or state*	Tend'ency,	*quality or state of* tending.
Ence		*of being.*	Ad her'ence,	*quality or state of* adhering.
Ude			Qui'et ude,	*state of being* quiet.
Ness	/		Rude'ness,	*state of being* rude.
Ment	}	*the act*	Move'ment,	*act of* moving.
Ure		*of.*	Seiz'ure,	*act of* seizing.

---

defined by such phrases as "*made of*," "*made into*," "*made, or formed like*," "*having*," "*affected by*," etc. The following are examples:—

Glob'ate, *formed like* a globe.
Silk'en, *made of* silk.
Re nown'ed, *having* renown.

[1] This affix has two other forms, Ety and Ty; as, in vari*ety* and novel*ty*.

SPELLING AND DICTATION. 39

Exercise 11.

Affixes.	Force.	Examples.	Definitions.
Al	⎫	Fa′ tal,	pertaining to fate.
Ern	⎪	East′ ern,	relating to the east.
Ic	⎪	He ro′ ic,	pertaining to a hero.
An	⎬ pertaining or	Af′ ri can,	pertaining to Africa.
Ine	⎪ relating to.	Ser′ pen tine,	pertaining to a serpent.
Ile	⎪	In′ fant ile,	pertaining to an infant.
Ar	⎪	Con′ sul ar,	relating to a consul.
Ical	⎭	Po et′ ic al,	relating to a poet.

Exercise 12.

Ous	⎫	Dan′ ger ous,	full of danger.
Ose	⎬ full of.	Ver bose′,	full of words.
Ful[1]	⎭	Hope′ ful,	full of hope.
Ly	manner.	Rude′ ly,	in a rude manner.
Able	⎰ that may or	Trace′ a ble,	that may be traced.
Ible	⎱ can be; fit to be.	Ed′ i ble,	fit to be eaten.

Exercise 13.

Age	the act of.	Cart′ age,	the act of carting.
Oid	⎰ having ⎱ form of.	Sphe′ roid,	having the form of a sphere.
Ism[2]	doctrine.	Mor′ mon ism,	doctrine of the Mormons.
Less	without.	Home′ less,	without a home.
Ish	somewhat.	New′ ish,	somewhat new.
Some	somewhat.	Lone′ some,	somewhat lonely.

---

[1] The affix Ful, when, with a radical, it forms a noun, signifies "*what*, or *as much as, will fill;*" that is, denotes the *amount* or *quantity* necessary to fill whatever is expressed by the radical: as, hand*ful*, *what*, or *as much as, will fill* the hand; arm*ful*, *what will fill* the arm.

[2] This affix deserves special notice. It marks *what is peculiar to* persons or things; and hence denotes a *doctrine* or *system*, a *state*, or *condition*, as also an *idiom* in language. Examples are:—

    Cal′ vin ism, *the doctrines peculiar to* Calvin.
    Sav′ ag ism, *the state or condition of* a savage.
    He′ bra ism, *what is peculiar to* Hebrew; an idiom.
    Her′ o ism, *what is peculiar to* a hero; valour.

Exercise 14.

Affixes.	Force.	Examples.	Definitions.
SHIP	state, or	LORD' SHIP,	the state of a lord.
HOOD	jurisdic-	CHILD' HOOD,	the state of being a child.
DOM	tion of.	POPE' DOM,	the jurisdiction of the Pope.
WARD	toward.	WEST' WARD,	toward the west.

KIN		LAMB' KIN,	a *little* lamb.
LING		GOS' LING,	a *little*, or *young* goose.
ULE		GLOB' ULE,	a *little* globe.
CULE	*little, petty,*	AN I MAL' CULE,	a *minute* animal.
CLE	*or minute.*	TU' BER CLE,	a *little* tumour.
ICLE		PAR' TI CLE,	a *minute* part.
OCK		HILL' OCK,	a *little* hill.
ET		FLOW' ER ET,	a *little* flower.
LET		RING' LET,	a *little* ring, or curl.

ROOTS, AND DERIVATIVES FORMED FROM THEM BY MEANS OF PREFIXES.

In the following exercises, each root or radical is combined with several prefixes. The prefix and the radical are first placed apart: the force of the radical rather than its precise definition being given. The two parts are then put together, and defined in connexion. The pupil should be questioned often on the parts separately, and required to spell and pronounce distinctly, here as everywhere else, each derivative, before giving its derivation.

The advantage of giving the English form assumed by the Latin word is manifest. If the pupil does not study Latin, the Latin form of the root is distracting, superfluous, and uninstructive; if he does study Latin, he can supply the Latin form for himself, and the comparison of the two will be found a good exercise.

SPELLING AND DICTATION. 41

Exercise 15.

Prefixes.	Roots.	Derivatives.	Definitions.
En	} ABLE, *strong.*	En a′ ble,	to make able.
Dis		Dis¹ a′ ble,	to deprive of ability.
Un		Un a′ ble,	not able.
Ad	} HERE, *to stick.*	Ad here′,²	to stick to; cling to.
Co		Co here′,	to stick together.
In		In here′,	to stick in; to exist in.
Com	} PLOT, *to scheme.*	Com plot′,	to plot together.
Counter		Coun′ ter plot,	plot against plot.
Under		Un′ der plot,	plot beneath.
Re	} PASS, *to step.*	Re pass′,	to pass again.
Sur³		Sur pass′,	to pass over; to excel.
Tres		Tres′ pass,	to pass beyond bounds.

Exercise 16.

E	} VADE, *to go.*	E vade′,	to go or get out; to avoid.
In		In vade′,	to go into; to attack.
Per		Per vade′,	to go, or pass through.
Counter	} VOTE, *to signify a choice; a suffrage.*	Coun′ ter vote,	opposite vote.
Over		O ver vote′,	to vote beyond.
Out		Out vote′,	to vote beyond.
De	} CLINE, *to lean.*	De cline′,	to lean down; to fail.
Re		Re cline′,	to lean back; to repose.
In		In cline′,	to lean into, or towards.
Bene	} FIT, *to make; to do.*	Ben′ e fit,	to do good, or well for.
Pro		Prof′ it,	to do, or act for; improve.
Re		Re fit′,	to make again; repair.

Exercise 17.

Com	} PRISE, *to take.*	Com prise′, to take together; include.
Enter⁴		En′ ter prise, take in (hand).

---

¹ Dis, in *disable* is *privative*. See remarks on Privatives, p. 37
² Note that the radical word HERE (*to stick*), though it appears in the derivative forms *Ad*here, *Co*here, and *In*here, can never be used alone, as an independent word. Radicals that are thus inseparable from prefixes or suffixes, are called INSEPARABLE RADICALS.
³ SUR is for *super* (*over*), and TRES for *trans* (*over*, *across*).
⁴ ENTER is for INTER, *between*, *among*, *within*, *in*.

Prefixes.	Roots.	Derivatives.	Definitions.
IN	} SPHERE, *a globe.*	IN SPHERE',	to place in a sphere.
HEMI		HEM' I SPHERE,	half a sphere.
SEMI		SEM' I SPHERE,	half a sphere. [der.
DI	} GRESS, *to go; act of going.*	DI GRESS',	to go aside from; wan-
CON		CON' GRESS,	a going together; coun-
PRO		PRO' GRESS,	to go forward. [cil.
TRANS		TRANS GRESS',	to go beyond bounds.

Exercise 18.

AD	} JACENT, *lying.*	AD JA' CENT,	lying near.
CIRCUM		CIR CUM JA' CENT,	lying around.
IN		IN JA' CENT,	lying in, or within.
SUB		SUB JA' CENT,	lying under.
AD	} JURE, *to swear.*	AD JURE',	to cause to swear to.
AB		AB JURE',	to swear off from.
CON		CON JURE',[1]	to swear together.
PER		PER JURE',	swear through, *i.e., falsely.*
AD	} JUDGE, *to pass sentence; to decide.*	AD JUDGE',	to judge to; to decide.
PRE		PRE JUDGE',	to judge beforehand.
MIS		MIS JUDGE',	to judge wrong.
FORE		FORE JUDGE',	to judge beforehand.

Exercise 19.

A[2]	} MOUNT, *to rise.*	A MOUNT',	to mount up to.
RE		RE MOUNT',	to mount again.
SUR		SUR MOUNT',	to mount over.
DIS		DIS MOUNT',	to get down; to alight.[3]
E	} MOTION, *movement; a moving.*	E MO' TION,	a moving (of the mind).[4]
COM		COM MO' TION,	a moving together.
PRO		PRO MO' TION,	a moving forwards.

---

[1] CON' JURE (*kun' jer*), with the accent on the first syllable, means to practise witchcraft.

[2] A is for AD (*to*), and SUR for SUPER (*above*).

[3] DIS, in *dis*mount, is *privative.* The full definition, therefore, would be, "*to take out of the state of*" being mounted.

[4] Literally, *an out-moving, i.e.,* an excitement, of the feelings.

| Prefixes. | Roots. | Derivatives. | Definitions. |

AT	TRIBUTE,	AT TRIB' UTE,	to give or grant to.
CON	to give; to	CON TRIB' UTE,	to give along with others.
DIS	grant.	DIS TRIB' UTE,	to give apart; deal out.

Exercise 20.

RE		RE CUR',	to run back (in thought).
CON	CUR,	CON CUR',	to run together; to agree.
IN	to run.	IN CUR',	to run into. [happen.
OC		OC CUR',	to run in the way of; to

| EX | CURSION, | EX CUR' SION, | a running out; ramble. |
| IN | the act of running. | IN CUR' SION, | a running into, or upon. |

EX		EX SCIND',	to cut out.
AB	SCIND,	AB SCIND',	to cut from, or off.
RE	to cut.	RE SCIND',	to cut off again; to repeal.

Exercise 21.

IN		IN CIS' ION,	a cutting into.
EX	CISION,	EX CIS' ION,	a cutting out. [ment.
DE	a cutting.	DE CIS' ION,	a cutting off; a settle-
PRE		PRE CIS' ION,[1]	a cutting off; accuracy.

AP		AP PEND',	to hang to.
DE	PEND,	DE PEND',	to hang down.
IM	to hang.	IM PEND',	to hang on, or over.
SUS		SUS PEND',	to hang up.

CON	VENE,	CON VENE',	to come together.
CONTRA	to	CON TRA VENE',	to come, or go against.
INTER	come.	IN TER VENE',	to come between.

Exercise 22.

CON		CON VEN' TION,	a coming together.
CIRCUM	VENTION,	CIR CUM VEN' TION,	a coming round, fraud.
IN	a coming.	IN VEN' TION,	a coming into (something
PRE		PRE VEN' TION,	a coming before. [new.)[2]

---

[1] PRECISION is, literally, *the act of cutting off before or in front*, and hence, generally, the act of cutting off needless parts, *i.e.*, *exactness*.

[2] That is, *the finding out* of new things.

SPELLING AND DICTATION.

Prefixes.	Roots.	Derivatives.	Definitions.
Dis	⎱ SECTION,	Dis sec′ tion,	a cutting apart.
Inter	⎰ *a cutting:* *a cut.*	In ter sec′ tion,	a cutting between.
In	⎫ TRUDE,	In trude′,	to push, or thrust into.
Pro	⎪ *to push,*	Pro trude′,	push, or thrust forward.
Ex	⎬ *or*	Ex trude′,	to push out or off.
Ob	⎭ *thrust.*	Ob trude′,	push towards; urge upon.

Exercise 23.

In	⎫ TRUSION,	In tru′ sion, the act of pushing into.
Pro	⎬ *the act of*	Pro tru′ sion, act of pushing forward.
Ex	⎭ *pushing.*	Ex tru′ sion, the act of pushing out.
Col	⎫ LOCUTION,	Col lo cu′ tion, a talking together.
Circum	⎬ *a speak-*	Cir cum lo cu′ tion, a talking round about.
E	⎭ *ing; talk.*	El o cu′ tion, a speaking out; delivery.
In	⎫ CUMBENT,	In cum′ bent, lying or resting in or on.
Re	⎬ *lying or*	Re cum′ bent, lying back; reclining.
Pro	⎭ *resting.*	Pro cum′ bent, lying or leaning forward.

Exercise 24.

Com	⎫		Com pose′,	to put together.
De	⎪		De pose′,	to put or lay down.
Inter	⎪		In ter pose′,	to put or place between.
Re	⎪	POSE,	Re pose′,	to put or lay back.
Ex	⎬	*to put,*	Ex pose′,	to put or lay out.
Im	⎪	*or*	Im pose′, to put in or upon; to deceive.
Dis	⎪	*place.*	Dis pose′,	to put or set apart.
Trans	⎪		Trans pose′,	to put across.[1]
Sup	⎪		Sup pose′,	to put under view.
Pro	⎭		Pro pose′,	to put before.
Con	⎫ STRUCT,	Con struct′,	to build together.
Re-con	⎬ *to build;*	Re-con struct′, to build together again.
Ob	⎭ *pile.*	Ob struct′,	to build or pile against.

---

[1] That is, to put each in the place of the other; to exchange the order of things.

Exercise 25.

Prefixes.	Roots.	Derivatives.	Definitions.
E	⎫ MIGRATE,	EM' I GRATE,	to travel out.
IM	⎬ *to go;*	IM' MI GRATE,	to travel into.
TRANS	⎭ *to travel.*	TRANS' MI GRATE,	to travel over or across.
EN	⎫	EN ACT',	to put into action.
COUNTER	⎪ ACT,	COUN TER ACT',	to act against.
OVER	⎬ *to do;*	O VER ACT',	to act beyond.
RE	⎪ *to move.*	RE ACT',	to act again, or back.
TRANS	⎭	TRANS ACT',	to act or do.
UN	⎫ NATURAL,	UN NAT' U RAL,	not natural.
SUPER	⎬ *pertaining*	SU PER NAT' U RAL,	above the natural.
PRETER	⎭ *to nature.*	PRE TER NAT' U RAL,	beyond the natural.

Exercise 26.

DE	⎫	DE JECT',	to cast down.
E	⎪	E JECT',	to cast out.
IN	⎪ JECT,	IN JECT',	to cast into.
OB	⎬ *to cast,*	OB JECT',	to cast in front; to oppose.
PRO	⎪ *or throw.*	PRO JECT',	to cast forward.
RE	⎪	RE JECT',	to cast back; to refuse.
SUB	⎭	SUB JECT',	to cast under; to subdue.
PRE	⎫ CEDE,	PRE CEDE',	to go before.
INTER	⎬ *to go or*	IN TER CEDE,	to go between.
RE	⎭ *come;*	RE CEDE',	to go back.

Exercise 27.

AC	⎫ CEDE, *to*	AC CEDE',	to go to; yield, assent to.
EX	⎪ *go or*	EX CEED',[1]	to go beyond.
PRO	⎬ *come;*	PRO CEED',[1]	to go forward; advance.
SUC	⎪ *to*	SUC CEED',[1]	to go or come after.
CON	⎭ *yield.*	CON CEDE',	to go with in opinion.

---

[1] Observe, that in the three words, Exceed, Proceed, and Succeed, the radical part is written *ceed*, instead of *cede*.

Prefixes.	Roots.	Derivatives.	Definitions.
Ac	⎫	Ac ces' sion,	a going to ; addition.
Con	⎪ cession,	Con ces' sion,	a going with ; yielding.
Inter	⎬ a going ;	In ter ces' sion,	a going between.
Se	⎪ a yield-	Se ces' sion,	a going aside or away.
Pro	⎪ ing.	Pro ces' sion,	a going forward.
Suc	⎭	Suc ces' sion,	a going after.

Exercise 28.

Re	⎫	Re duce',	to lead back; to bring down.
De	⎪	De duce',	to lead or draw from ; to infer
Pro	⎪ duce, to	Pro duce',	to lead or bring forth.
Se	⎬ lead or	Se duce',	to lead away; to corrupt.
In	⎪ draw.	In duce',	to lead into ; to persuade.
E	⎪	E duce',	to lead or bring out.
Ad	⎪	Ad duce',	to lead or bring to.
Con	⎭	Con duce',	to lead together ; to tend.

Exercise 29.

As	⎫	As sist',	to stand to ; to aid.
Con	⎪	Con sist',	to stand together.
Re	⎪	Re sist',	to stand against ; to oppose.
De	⎬ sist, to	De sist',	to stand off from ; to cease.
In	⎪ stand.	In sist',	to stand upon ; to urge.
Ex	⎪	Ex[1] ist',	to stand out ; *i.e.*, to be.
Sub	⎪	Sub sist',	to stand under ; to be.
Per	⎭	Per sist',	to stand through; persevere.

Sub	⎫ scribe,	Sub scribe',	to write one's name under
Circum	⎪ to	Cir cum scribe',	to mark around ; limit.
Pre	⎬ write ;	Pre scribe',	write or mark down be
In	⎪ to	In scribe',	to write upon. [fore
De	⎭ mark.	De scribe',	write down ; delineate.

---

[1] Notice that the letter *s*, in the radical, sist, is omitted or absorbed, when the prefix Ex is united with it.

SPELLING AND DICTATION.

Exercise 30.

Prefixes.	Roots.	Derivatives.	Definitions.
AT		AT TRACT',	to draw to, or towards.
CON		CON TRACT',	to draw together.
ABS		ABS TRACT',	to draw, or take from.
EX	TRACT, to	EX TRACT',	to draw, or take out.
PRO	draw.	PRO TRACT',	to draw, or bring forward.
SUB		SUB TRACT',	to draw from beneath.
DE		DE TRACT',	to draw, or take from.
DIS		DIS TRACT',	to draw apart; to confuse.
CON		CON FUSE',	to pour together; perplex.
RE		RE FUSE',	to pour back; to reject.
IN	FUSE, to	IN FUSE',	to pour into.
TRANS	melt.	TRANS FUSE',	to pour through.
SUF		SUF FUSE',	to pour beneath.
DIF		DIF FUSE',	to pour apart; to spread.

Exercise 31.

IN		IN VOLVE',	to roll in; to comprise.
E	VOLVE, to	E VOLVE',	to roll out; to disclose.
DE	roll.	DE VOLVE',	to roll down; to fall to.
RE		RE VOLVE',	to roll again; turn round.
IN		IN VO LU' TION,	a rolling in; involving.
E	VOLUTION,	EV O LU' TION,	a rolling out; evolving.
RE	a rolling.	RE VO LU' TION,	rolling again; revolving.
CON		CON VO LU TION',	a rolling together.

Exercise 32.

DE		DE PRESS',	to press down.
IM		IM PRESS',	to press on or upon.
COM	PRESS, to	COM PRESS',	to press together.
RE	squeeze;	RE PRESS',	to press back.
EX	to urge.	EX PRESS',	to press out.
OP		OP PRESS',	to press against.
SUP		SUP PRESS',	to press under; to crush.

Prefixes.	Roots.	Derivatives.	Definitions.
Af		Af fix',	to fix to.
Suf	fix, to	Suf fix',	to fix after.
Pre	fasten;	Pre fix',	to fix before.
Post	to set.	Post fix',	to fix after.
Trans		Trans fix',	to fix through.

Exercise 33.

In		In spect',	to look into.
Pro		Pros' pect,	a look or view ahead.
Intro	spect, look.	In tro spect',	to look within.
Re		Re spect',	to look to again; regard.
Ex		Ex pect',[1]	to look out for; to wait for.
Con	flux, a	Con' flux,	a flowing together.
Re	flow, or	Re' flux,	a flowing back.
In	flowing.	In' flux,	a flowing in.
Con	fluent,	Con' flu ent,	flowing together.
Re	flowing.	Ref' lu ent,	flowing back.

Exercise 34.

Con		Con fer',	to bring together (counsels).
Of		Of' fer,	to bring in the way of.
Pre		Pre fer',	to bear before, *i.e., choose.*
Dif	fer,	Dif' fer,	to bear apart; disagree.
Re	to bear,	Re fer',	to bear back for decision.
Trans	to bring.	Trans fer',	to bear over; to remove.
In		In fer',	to bring in (a conclusion).
Suf		Suf' fer,	to bear under; to endure.
De		De fer',	to bear off; to delay.
Re	mit,	Re mit',	to send back.
Trans	to send,	Trans mit',	to send across, or over.
Per	to let	Per mit',	to send through; to allow.
Ad	go.	Ad mit',	to send to, or let go in.

---

[1] See Note, p. 46.

Exercise 35.

Prefixes.	Roots.	Derivatives.	Definitions.
DE		DE MIS' SION,	a sending down.
E	MISSION,	E MIS' SION,	a sending out. [pause.
INTER	a send-	IN TER MIS' SION,	a sending between, a
AD	ing.	AD MIS' SION,	a letting (one) go to.
SUB		SUB MIS' SION,	a sending under.
AT		AT TAIN',	to reach to; to get.
DE		DE TAIN',	to hold off.
PER	TAIN,	PER TAIN',	to hold through; to be-
CON	to hold,	CON TAIN',	to hold together. [long.
RE	to	RE TAIN',	to hold or keep back.
SUS	reach.	SUS TAIN',	to hold up; to support.
ENTER[1]		EN TER TAIN',	to hold or keep between
OB		OB TAIN',	to hold; to get; to gain.

Exercise 36.

AD		AD VERT',	to turn to; refer to.
RE		RE VERT',	to turn back.
DI	VERT,	DI VERT',	to turn aside, or away.
A	to	A VERT',	to turn from, or away.
SUB	turn.	SUB VERT',	to turn under; to overthrow.
PER		PER VERT',	to turn thoroughly.
CON		CON VERT',	to turn altogether; to change.
RE	VERSE,	RE VERSE',	to turn back.
CON	to	CON VERSE',	to turn, or exchange (words).
PER	turn;	PER VERSE',	turned thoroughly (in a bad
A	turned.	A VERSE',	turned from. direction)

[1] ENTER is for *Inter*.

DERIVATIVES MADE OPPOSITES BY PREFIXES.

In this Section, each root is combined with two prefixes of opposite meaning; by which means the derivatives also become opposites.

Exercise 37.

Prefixes.	Roots.	Derivatives.	Definitions.
ANTE POST	DATE, *to note time.*	AN' TE DATE, POST' DATE,	to date before. to date after.
AD A	VERT, *to turn.*	AD VERT', A VERT',	to turn to. to turn from or [away.
IN E	GRESS, *a going.*	IN' GRESS, E' GRESS,	a going in. a going out.
IN EX	HALE, *to breathe.*	IN HALE', EX HALE',	to breathe in. to breathe out.
ANTI SYM	PATHY, *feeling.*	AN TIP' A THY, SYM' PA THY,	a feeling against. a feeling with.

Exercise 38.

BENE MALE	FACTOR, *a doer.*	BEN E FAC' TOR, MAL E FAC' TOR,	a well-doer. an evil-doer.
E IM	MIGRATE, *to travel.*	EM' I GRATE, IM' MI GRATE,	to travel out. to travel into.
E IN	JECT, *to cast.*	E JECT', IN JECT',	to cast out. to cast in.
IN EX	CLUDE, *to shut.*	IN CLUDE', EX CLUDE',	to shut in. to shut out.

Exercise 39.

IM EX	PORT, *to carry.*	IM PORT', EX PORT',	to carry in. to carry out.
IN EF	FUSE, *to pour.*	IN FUSE', EF FUSE',	to pour in. to pour out.

SPELLING AND DICTATION.

Prefixes	Roots.	Derivatives.	Definitions.
Pro	} Pel, *to drive.*	Pro pel′,	to drive forward.
Re		Re pel′,	to drive back.
En	} Robe, *a gown.*	En robe′,	to put on a robe.
Dis		Dis robe′,	to take off a robe.

Exercise 40.

Pro	} Spect, *to look;*	Pros′ pect,	a looking forward.
Retro	*a looking.*	Ret′ ro spect,	a looking back.
Bene	} Volent, *wish-*	Be nev′ o lent,	well-wishing.
Male	*ing.*	Ma lev′ o lent,	ill-wishing.
Dys	} Pepsy, *diges-*	Dys pep′ sy,	bad digestion.
Eu	*tion.*	Eu pep′ sy,	good digestion.
Con	} Fluent, *flow-*	Con′ fluent,	flowing together.
Dif	*ing.*	Dif′ flu ent,	flowing apart.
Ante	} Diluvian, *relat-*	An te di lu′ vi an,	before the flood.
Post	*ing to the flood.*	Post di lu′ vi an,	after the flood.

ROOTS AND DERIVATIVES FORMED FROM THEM BY MEANS OF AFFIXES.

In this section the roots are united with a variety of *affixes*. The meaning of each root or radical is given separately, while that of the affix, as in the preceding section, is presented in the definition of the derivative with which it is combined. The pupil ought, however, occasionally to revise the Section in which the affixes are explained in detail.

Exercise 41.

Roots.	Affixes.	Derivatives.	Definitions.
Ign, *fire.*	{ eous	Ig′ ne ous	having the nature of fire.
	ite[1]	Ig nite′,	to take fire.
	ition	Ig ni′ tion,	act of taking fire.
	itible	Ig nit′ i ble,	that may be ignited.

---

[1] The affix Ite has the same meaning as Ate. See note, p. 37.

Roots.	Affixes.	Derivatives.	Definitions.
Vitr, glass.	eous	Vit' re ous,	of the nature of glass.
	eousness	Vit' re ous ness,	quality of being vitreous.
	ify	Vit' ri fy,	to change into glass.
	ifiable	Vit' ri fi a ble,	that may be turned into glass.

Exercise 42.

	ed	Act',	to do.
Act, to do.	ive	Act' ive,	tending to act; nimble.
	ively	Act' ive ly,	in an active manner.
	ivity	Ac tiv' i ty,	quality of being active.
	or	Act' or,	one who acts.
	ress	Act' ress,	female that acts.
	uate	Act' u ate,	to make, or cause to act.
	ual	Act' u al,	relating to the act; real.

Exercise 43.

	al	Dent' al,	relating to the teeth.
Dent,[1] a tooth, a mark as of a tooth.	ate	Dent' ate,	made, or pointed like teeth.
	ated[2]	Dent' a ted,	made, or pointed like teeth.
	ed	Dent' ed,	having dents or notches.
	icle	Dent' i cle,	a small tooth.
	ist	Dent' ist,	a doctor for the teeth.
	istry	Dent' is try,	the practice of a dentist.
	ition	Dent i' tion,	the act of forming teeth.

Exercise 44.

	aceous	Herb a' ceous,	of the nature of an herb.
Herb, a plant, a vegetable.	al	Herb' al,	pertaining to herbs.
	alist	Herb' al ist,	one skilled in herbs.
	ary	Herb' a ry,	a place where herbs grow.
	ist	Herb' ist,	one skilled in herbs.
	age	Herb' age,	herbs taken collectively.
	less	Herb' less,	without herbs.

[1] Dent, when used alone, means, "*to mark as with a tooth; to make a small hollow or notch.*"

[2] Ated is a compound affix, made up of Ate and Ed. One of them is here merely euphonic: dent*ated*, meaning the same as dent*ate*.

COMPOUND WORDS MADE UP OF TWO ROOTS.

In this section the compound words are first separated into the simple words composing them: the meaning of each part respectively being placed under each in *italics*. The two parts are then put together again, and defined, as one word.

Exercise 45.

1st Part.	2d Part.	Compounds.	Definitions.
DEM, *people.*	AGOGUE, *a leader.*	DEM' A GOGUE,	a factious leader of the people.
PED, *child.*		PED' A GOGUE,	leader of children; a schoolmaster.
SOMN, *sleep.*	AMBULIST, *a walker.*	SOM NAM' BU LIST,	a sleep-walker.
PHIL, *love.*	ANTHROPY, *mankind.*	PHI LAN' THRO PY,	love of mankind.
MIS, *hatred.*		MIS AN' THRO PY,	hatred of mankind.
MON, *one.*	ARCHY, *government.*	MON' ARCH Y,	government of one person.
OLIG, *few.*		OL' I GARCH Y,	government of a few.

Exercise 46.

AGRI, *field.*	CULTURE, *tillage.*	AG' RI CUL TURE,	tillage of fields; farming.
HORTI, *garden.*		HOR' TI CUL TURE,	culture of a garden, gardening.
MEGA, *big.*	COSM, *world.*	MEG' A COSM,	a great world.
MICRO, *little.*		MI' CRO COSM,	a little world.
MONO, *one.*	CHORD, *string.*	MON' O CHORD,	a musical instrument having one string.
POLY, *many.*		POL' Y CHORD,	having many chords. or strings.

Exercise 47.

1st Part.	2d Part.	Compounds.	Definitions.
HOMI, man.		HOM' I CIDE,	the killing of a man.
PARRI, parent.		PAR' RI CIDE,	the killing of a parent.
INFANTI, infant.		IN FANT' I CIDE,	the killing of an infant.
MATRI, mother.	CIDE, a killing.	MAT' RI CIDE,	the killing of a mother.
FRATRI, brother.		FRAT' RI CIDE,	the killing of a brother.
REGI, king.		REG' I CIDE,	the killing of a king.
SUI, self.		SU' I CIDE,	the killing of one's-self.

Exercise 48.

DEMO, people.	CRACY, rule.	DE MOC' RA CY,	rule of the people.
ARISTO, noble.		AR IS TOC' RA CY,	rule of the nobles.
ORTHO, right.	DOX, doctrine.	OR' THO DOX,	right in doctrine.
HETERO, other.		HET' E RO DOX,	other, or different in doctrine.
HIPPO, horse.	DROME, course.	HIP' PO DROME,	horse-course, race-course.
AQUE, water.	DUCT, tube or channel.	AQ' UE DUCT,	artificial channel for water.

Exercise 49.

TRI, three.		TRI EN' NI AL,	pertaining to three years.
SEPT, seven.	ENNIAL, year or yearly.	SEP TEN' NI AL,	pertaining to seven years.
CENT, hundred.		CEN TEN' NI AL,	pertaining to a hundred years.
MILL, thousand.		MIL LEN' NI AL,	pertaining to a thousand years.

SPELLING AND DICTATION.

1st Part.	2d Part.	Compounds.	Definitions.
Odori, scent.	} FEROUS, bearing. {	O do rif' er ous,	bearing, or yielding odour.
Auri, gold.		Au rif' er ous,	bearing, or yielding gold.
Argenti, silver.		Ar gent if' er ous,	bearing, or yielding silver.

Exercise 50.

1st Part.	2d Part.	Compounds.	Definitions.
Stupe, stupid.	} FACTION, act of making. {	Stu pe fac' tion,	act of making stupid; stupidity.
Putre, rotten.		Pu tre fac' tion,	act of making or becoming rotten.
Denti, tooth.	} FRICE, rubbing. {	Dent' i frice,	preparation to rub or clean the teeth.
Cruci, cross.	} FORM, shape. {	Cru' ci form,	having the form of a cross.
Melli, honey.	} {	Mel lif' lu ous,	flowing with honey; sweet.
Bi, two.	} GAMY, marriage. {	Big' a my,	the having of two wives or husbands.
Poly, many.		Po lyg' a my,	plurality of wives or husbands.

Exercise 51.

1st Part.	2d Part.	Compounds.	Definitions.
Hexa, six.	} GON, angle. {	Hex' a gon,	a figure having six angles and sides.
Octa, eight.		Oc' ta gon,	a figure having eight sides.
Poly, many.		Pol' y gon,	a figure having many angles.
Poly, many.	} GLOT, tongue. {	Pol' y glot,	containing many tongues.
Homo, same.	} GENEOUS, having the nature. {	Ho mo ge' ne ous,	having the same nature.
Hetero, other.		Het e ro ge' ne ous,	having a different nature.

SPELLING AND DICTATION.

Exercise 52.

1st Part.	2d Part,	Compounds.	Definitions.
Auto, *self.*	GRAPH, *writing or marking.*	Au'to graph,	the handwriting of one's-self.
Tele, *far off.*		Tel'e graph,	a contrivance to convey news far off.
Grandi, *grand.*	loquence, *talk.*	Gran dil'o quence,	great talk; lofty speaking.
Bio, *life.*		Bi og'ra phy,	a writing, or history of one's-self.
Steno, *short.*		Ste nog'ra phy,	short-hand writing.
Typo, *type.*	GRAPHY, *a writing, marking, description.*	Ty pog'ra phy,	a marking with types; printing.
Topo, *place.*		To pog'ra phy,	a description of places.
Geo, *earth.*		Ge og'ra phy,	a description of the earth.
Litho, *stone.*		Li thog'ra phy,	art of marking or engraving on stone.
Ortho, *right.*		Or thog'ra phy,	correct writing; spelling.

Exercise 53.

Geo, *earth.*		Ge ol'o gy,	science of the formation of the earth.
Zoo, *animal.*	LOGY, *word, reason, science.*	Zo ol'o gy,	science of animals.
Theo, *God.*		The ol'o gy,	the science which treats of God.
Concho, *shell.*		Conch ol'o gy,	science of shells.
Chrono, *time.*		Chro nol'o gy,	science of computing time or dates.
Equi, *equal.*	LATERAL, *pertaining to the side.*	E qui lat'er al,	having equal sides.
Quadri, *four.*		Quad ri lat'er al,	having four sides.
Multi, *many.*		Mul ti lat'er al,	having many sides.

SPELLING AND DICTATION.

Exercise 54.

1st Part.	2d Part.	Compounds.	Definitions.
SOLI, alone.	LOQUY, talk.	SO LIL' O QUY,	talking alone, or by one's-self.
IDO, image.	LATRY, worship.	I DOL' A TRY,	worship of idols.
MONO, one.	LOGUE, discourse,	MON' O LOGUE,	discourse to one's-self; soliloquy.
DECA, ten.	command-ment.	DEC' A LOGUE,	the ten commandments.

Exercise 55.

AERO, air.		A ER OM' E TER,	an instrument for measuring the air.
CHRONO, time.	METER, a measure.	CHRO NOM' E TER,	an instrument for measuring time.
BARO, weight.		BAROM' E TER,	measurer of the weight of the air.
THERMO, heat.		THER MOM' E TER,	measurer of heat.
LOGO, word.	MACHY, fight.	LO GOM' A CHY,	fight, or war of words.
COSMO, world.	POLITE, citizen.	COS MOP' O LITE,	a citizen of the world.
AERO, air.	NAUT, one who sails.	A' ER O NAUT,	one who sails in or navigates the air.
POLY, many.	NESIA, islands.	POL Y NE' SIA,[1]	consisting of many islands.

Exercise 56.

ASTRO, star.		AS TRON' O MY,	law, or science of the stars.
ECO, house.	NOMY, law.	E CON' O MY,	law, or rule of a house; thriftiness.
DEUTERO, second.		DEU TER ON' O MY,	second law (or fifth book) of Moses.

---

[1] This is a term in geography, used to designate numerous groups of islands in the Pacific Ocean.

SPELLING AND DICTATION.

1st Part.	2d Part.	Compounds.	Definitions.
PSALM, psalm.	ODY, a song, or a singing.	PSALM' O DY,	singing, or the art of singing psalms.
PAN, all.	ORAMA, view.	PAN O RA' MA,	a complete view; view of all.
COSM, world.		COS' MO RA' MA,	view of the world.
DI, two.	PHTHONG, sound.	DIPH' THONG,	union of two vowels in one sound.
TRI, three.		TRIPH' THONG,	union of three vowels in one syllable.
DU, two.	PLICATE, fold.	DU' PLI CATE,	two-fold; double.
OMNI, all.	POTENT, having power.	OM NIP' O TENT,	having all power.

Exercise 57.

OVI, egg.	PAROUS, producing.	O VIP' A ROUS,	producing eggs.
VERMI, worm.		VER MIP' A ROUS,	producing worms.
CYCLO, circle.	PEDIA, instruction.	CY CLO PE' DI A,	circle of instruction in the arts and sciences.
QUADRU, four.	PED, a foot.	QUAD' RU PED,	a four-footed animal.
CENTI, hundred.		CEN' TI PED,	hundred-footed.
HYDRO, water.	PHOBIA, dread.	HY DRO PHO' BI A,	dread of water; canine madness.
HIPPO, horse.	POTAMUS, river.	HIP PO POT' A MUS,	a river-horse.

Exercise 58.

TELE, far off.	SCOPE, a view or sight.	TEL' E SCOPE,	instrument for viewing things far off.
MICRO, small.		MI' CRO SCOPE,	instrument for viewing things minute.

SPELLING AND DICTATION. 59

1st Part.	2d Part.	Compounds.	Definitions.
Sol, *sun.*	STICE, *a standing.*	Sol′ stice,	standing still of the sun.
Armi, *arms.*		Arm′ is tice,	a standing still of arms; truce.
Philo, *love.*	sophy, *wisdom.*	Phi los′ o phy,	love of wisdom; knowledge.
Mono, *one.*	theism, *belief in a God.*	Mon′ o the ism,	belief in one God only.
Poly, *many.*		Pol′ y the ism,	belief in many Gods.

Exercise 59.

Pyro, *fire.*	technic, *relating to art.*	Py ro tech′ nic,	relating to the art of making fire-works.
Poly, *many.*		Pol y tech′ nic,	relating to many arts.
Proto, *first.*	type, *mark, emblem.*	Pro′ to type,	first-type; original pattern or model.
Stereo, *solid.*		Ste′ re o type,	solid type; plate of metallic type.
Carni, *flesh.*	vorous, *eating or devouring.*	Car niv′ o rous,	flesh-eating, or devouring.
Grani, *grain.*		Gra niv′ o rous,	grain-eating, or devouring.
Herbi, *herb.*		Herb iv′ o rous,	herb-eating, or devouring.

SECOND PART.

MISCELLANEOUS DICTATION EXERCISES.[1]

I. PROVERBS.

A lean fee is a fit reward for a lazy clerk. Birds of a feather will flock together. Credit ought rather to be given to the eyes than to the ears. Empty vessels make the greatest sound. Fire and water are good servants but bad masters. He that goes a-borrowing goes a-sorrowing. Make hay while the sun shines. Little spoken is soon amended.

II. PROVERBS

Learning is the eye of the mind. One bird in the hand is worth two in the bush. Quick promisers are slow performers. 'Tis too late to spare when all is spent. Heaven helps those who help themselves. He who is only his own pupil has a fool for his tutor. He that is well sheltered is a fool if he stir out into the rain. He that lives not well one year sorrows for it seven. He that knoweth useful things, not he that knows many things is the wise man.

III. PROVERBS.

He that looks for a requital serves himself, not me. He that loves himself too much loves an ill man. Rolling stones gather no moss. Saving is getting. Scandal will rub out like dirt when it is dry. Seek till you find and you'll not lose your labour. The way to avoid great faults is to beware of less. "They say so" is half a lie. Fortune gives her hand to a brave man. Friendship is not to be bought at a fair. A man may buy even gold too dear. He that will not be ruled by the rudder must be ruled by the rock.

---

[1] Punctuation rules are not attempted. A few directions from the teacher and much practice best teach this subject. The pupil should be instructed to err on the side of too few rather than too many points.

IV. ON PROVERBS.

The fact that they please the people, and have pleased them for ages; that they possess so vigorous a principle of life as to have maintained their ground ever new and ever young through all the centuries of a nation's existence; nay, that many of them have pleased not one nation only but many, so that they have made themselves a home in the most different lands; and further, that they have, not a few of them, come down to us from remotest antiquity, borne safely upon the waters of that great stream of time, which has swallowed so much beneath its waves,—all this, I think, may well make us pause should we be tempted to turn away from them with anything of indifference or disdain. ARCHBISHOP TRENCH.

V. THE BOY AND THE NETTLE.

A boy playing in the fields was stung by a nettle. He ran home to his mother, and told her that he had but touched the nasty weed and it had stung him. "It was your just touching it, my boy," said the mother, "that caused it to sting you. The next time you meddle with a nettle grasp it tightly, and it will not hurt you."

Do vigorously what you do at all.

VI. WHAT IS RICE?

The Rice plant is a species of grass growing very much like our own oats. When ripe, each grain is enclosed in a yellow husk, and hung in fine clusters on very thin stalks. It grows best in very moist soil, and low lands which are flooded at particular seasons are on that account preferred for its cultivation. Before it is used for food, the husk is removed by rubbing the grain between flat stones and blowing the broken husks away. Machines are also used for the same purpose. In our own country rice serves us for puddings, and for thickening soup, and is both cheap and wholesome.

VII. WHAT IS SAGO?

Sago, which is used extensively in this country, and brought from some islands of the Indian Ocean, is procured from the pith of a beautiful palm tree, and its shape, as known to us here, is caused by its being shaken through a sieve made of the fibres of palm leaves, while its glossy look is the result of drying over a charcoal fire. Sago is cheap and nourishing food, excellent for sick people and young children.

VIII. THE TWO PATHS.

Ask yourselves what is the leading motive which actuates you while you are at work. I do not ask what your leading motive is for working—that is a different thing. You may have families to support, parents to help, brides to win; you may have all these, or other such sacred and pre-eminent motives, to press the morning's labour, and prompt the twilight thought. But when you are fairly *at* the work, what is the motive which tells upon every touch of it? RUSKIN.

IX. THE CRAB AND HER MOTHER.

Said an old crab to a young one, "Why do you walk so crookedly, child? Walk straight!" "Mother," said the young crab, "show me the way, will you? and when I see you taking a straight course, I will try and follow."
Example is better than precept.

X. THE WAR-HORSE.

The fiery courser, when he hears from far
The sprightly trumpets and the shouts of war,
Pricks up his ears, and, trembling with delight,
Shifts place, and paws, and hopes the promised fight:
On his right shoulder his thick mane reclined,
Ruffles at speed, and dances in the wind;

Eager he stands, then, starting with a bound,
He spurns the turf and shakes the solid ground;
Fire from his eyes, clouds from his nostrils flow,
He bears his rider headlong on the foe!

DRYDEN.

XI. THE KING AND THE STABLE-BOY.

A king walking out one morning, met a lad at the stable-door, and asked him, "Well, boy, what do you do? What do they pay you?" "I help in the stables," replied the lad; "but I have nothing except victuals and clothes." "Be content," replied the king, "I have no more."

XII. HOW TO WIN.

A man who is very rich now was very poor when he was a boy. When asked how he got his riches, he replied— "My father taught me never to play till my work was finished, and never to spend money till I had earned it. If I had but half an hour's work to do in a day, I must do that the first thing, and in half an hour. After this I was allowed to play; and I could then play with much more pleasure than if I had the thought of an unfinished task before my mind. I early formed the habit of doing everything in its time, and it soon became perfectly easy to do so. To this habit I owe my prosperity."

Let every one who reads this go and do likewise, and he will meet a similar reward.

XIII. COCOA.

Cacao is the seed of a tree which abounds in the West Indies, and in several parts of South America, particularly on the Magdalena and in Guiana. These seeds or nuts are contained in pods resembling cucumbers, from twenty to thirty of them being closely packed in each. They are not unlike almonds in shape and size. The kernel, simply ground, is the cacao, or cocoa, as it is called, of the shops; when made into a paste, with sugar and vanilla, it is called chocolate, after the Mexican name of the tree, chocolatt.

XIV. WHALEBONE—GLUE—INK.

Whalebone is a substance very nearly resembling horn, and is obtained from the upper jaw of the whale. It appears to serve the animal instead of teeth. The pieces vary with the size of the whale—being from three to twelve feet in length, and, when very large, about one foot broad at the thickest end. It is used for umbrellas, parasols, stays, hoops, etc. etc.

GLUE.—Glue is made of refuse horns, hoofs, parings of hides, and other similar materials, boiled down to a thick jelly, and repeatedly strained so as to free it from all impurities. When cold, it makes hard brittle cakes.

INK.—The chief ingredients in most writing-inks are *galls* and *sulphate of iron*, with the addition of *gum arabic* to render the liquid adhesive, and make it flow freely from the pen.

XV. CHAUCER.

Geoffrey Chaucer is called the father of English poetry, because he is the first poet of note who wrote in the English language. Before his time, little had been written in English worthy of the name of poetry. Chaucer was born about the year 1328, in London. He studied at Cambridge, was a soldier and courtier, having the confidence of his king, Edward the Third. He lived in troublous times, but seems to have escaped any greater suffering than occasional imprisonment. He died in 1400, and was buried in Westminster Abbey, where his tomb may be seen. His chief poem is called the *Canterbury Tales*. A number of pilgrims journeying together to Canterbury beguile the time by telling tales. The description of these pilgrims gives us a curious picture of English life five hundred years ago. They are written in old English, and cannot be read without difficulty; but any one overcoming this will be greatly rewarded. There is a curious description of Chaucer written by another English poet a hundred years later, which gives some idea of Chaucer's appearance, and the costume of the time in which he lived.

XVI. VERSES ON CHAUCER.

His stature was not very tall;
Lean he was, his legs were small,
Hosed within a stock of red;
A button'd bonnet on his head,
From under which did hang, I ween,
Silver hairs both bright and sheen;
His beard was white, trimm'd round,
His countenance blithe and merry found.
A sleeveless jacket, large and wide,
With many plaits and skirts beside
Of water camlet did he wear;
A whittle[1] by his belt he bare.
His shoes were corned, broad before;
His inkhorn at his side he wore,
And in his hand he bore a book,
Thus did this ancient poet look.

XVII. THE VICAR.

I had scarce taken orders a year before I began to think seriously of matrimony, and chose my wife as she did her wedding-gown—not for a fine glossy surface, but such qualities as would wear well. To do her justice, she was a good-natured, notable woman, and as for education, there were few country ladies who could show more. She could read any English book without much spelling; but for pickling, preserving, and cookery, none could excel her. She prided herself also upon being an excellent contriver in housekeeping; though I could never find that we grew richer with all her contrivances.

However, we loved each other tenderly, and our fondness increased as we grew old. There was, in fact, nothing that could make us angry with the world or each other. We had an elegant house, situate in a fine country, and a

---

[1] Small sword.

good neighbourhood. The year was spent in moral or rural amusements, in visiting our rich neighbours, and relieving such as were poor. We had no revolutions to fear, nor fatigues to undergo; all our adventures were by the fireside, and all our migrations from the blue bed to the brown.—*From the Vicar of Wakefield.*

XVIII. ISAAC ASHFORD.

Next to these ladies, but in nought allied,
A noble peasant, Isaac Ashford, died.
Noble he was, contemning all things mean,
His truth unquestion'd and his soul serene:
Of no man's presence Isaac felt afraid;
At no man's question Isaac looked dismayed:
Shame knew him not, he dreaded no disgrace;
Truth, simple truth, was written in his face.
Yet while the serious thought his soul approved,
Cheerful he seem'd, and gentleness he loved:
To bliss domestic he his heart resign'd,
And, with the firmest, had the fondest mind:
Were others joyful, he looked smiling on,
And gave allowance where he needed none;
Good he refused with future ill to buy,
Nor knew a joy that caused reflection's sigh;
A friend to virtue, his unclouded breast
No envy stung, no jealousy distress'd;
(Bane of the poor! it wounds their weaker mind
To miss one favour which their neighbours find:)
Yet far was he from stoic pride removed;
He felt humanely and he warmly loved.—CRABBE.

XIX. INDIA-RUBBER.

Caoutchouc, or India-rubber, is obtained from the milky juice of various intertropical plants. Either the juice is applied to lumps of clay, and allowed to dry, coating after coating, till the requisite thickness is obtained, when the clay inside is crushed, and shaken out by an orifice left for that purpose; or it is coagulated by an acid, in which case the solid part is the caoutchouc. Most of the caoutchouc in Great Britain is brought from Para, Brazil, where the Indians used to make it into waterproof boots, long before the chemists of Europe found out a method of liquefying it, and so of making waterproof cloth.

Gutta Percha is the dried sap of a tree found in Malacca.

XX. TEA.

Tea is the dried leaves of a shrub grown chiefly in China and Japan, of which countries it is a native. It is an evergreen, grows to the height of from four to six feet, and bears pretty white flowers resembling wild-roses.

In China there are a great many tea-farms, generally of small extent, situated in the upper valleys and on the sloping sides of the hills, where the soil is light, rich, and well-drained. The plants are raised from seed, and they are generally allowed to remain three years in the ground before a crop of leaves is taken from them. They last about eight or ten years. When the crop is ready the leaves are carefully picked by hand, one by one. There are generally three or four gatherings each year, the first crop of young leaves in the spring being of the most value. A well-grown bush, well-treated, will produce two or three pounds of tea annually.

Tea was first brought to Europe by the Dutch East India Company in 1610, and must have been in use in England prior to 1660.

XXI. COFFEE.

Coffee is an evergreen shrub indigenous to the table-lands of Ethiopia. Its berries contain the coffee of commerce, called coffee-beans. The finest quality of coffee is produced in Arabia; but the largest quantities are exported by Brazil and Java.

Elevated situations are best suited for the growth of coffee. The trees are raised from slips, which are allowed four or five years to grow before the berries are gathered. They attain the height of eight or ten feet, and continue to bear fruit for from thirty to fifty years. They resemble a handsome laurel, and bear a profusion of clusters of fragrant white flowers, succeeded by brilliant red berries, sweet and pulpy, which ripen to a purple colour, each containing two coffee seeds or stones.

Coffee was used in England some years before tea was introduced.

XXII. THE NUT: A FABLE.

Two boys were once playing under a tree, when a nut fell from it near them. One of them picked it up. The other boy said: "It is my nut, for I saw it fall."

"No, it is mine," said the other, "for I picked it up."

Just then a bigger boy came along, and he said: "What are you disputing about?"

The little boys told him.

"Give it to me," said he, "and I will decide your quarrel for you."

So he cracked the nut, and gave one-half of the shell to one boy, saying: "This is for you, because you saw the nut fall." He then gave the other half-shell to the second boy, saying, "This is yours, because you picked up the nut." Then, putting the kernel into his own mouth, he said: "And this is for my trouble in cracking it."

XXIII. MAIZE.

Maize or Indian Corn is much larger than any grain which grows here. It has a stem as thick as a broom-handle, often eight feet high, and bearing the corn in ears of considerable size called cobs. The cobs are enclosed in a large leafy sheath, which is used for making paper in the United States; and some of you may have seen chests of oranges and lemons at the grocers' doors in this country, every orange wrapped in one of these sheaths to keep it dry and sound. These oranges have probably come from Spain or Sicily, where the Indian corn is also grown.

XXIV. ROBIN REDBREAST.

Good-bye, good-bye to summer!
   For summer's nearly done,
The garden smiling faintly
   Cool breezes in the sun.
Our thrushes now are silent,
   Our swallows flown away,—
But Robin's here in coat of brown
   And scarlet breast-knot gay.
Robin, Robin Redbreast,
   O Robin dear!
Robin sings so sweetly
   In the falling of the year.

ALLINGHAM.

XXV. SUGAR.

Sugar is a sweet crystallized substance obtained from the juice of the Sugar-Cane, a reed-like plant growing in most hot climates, but supposed to be originally a native of the East.

The root of the cane is jointed, and sends up several stems which are also jointed, and which rise to a height ranging from eight to twenty feet. A leaf three or four feet long springs from each joint, the flowers, which are whitish, and enveloped in long down, grow in bunches at the top of the cane.

When the canes are ripe, which is generally in February, March, and April, they are cut down close to the root, the leaves are stripped, the stalks are divided into convenient lengths, and taken at once to the crushing-mill. Here they are squeezed between iron rollers, and the juice flows, after passing through a strainer, into large clarifying vessels. After this the juice is several times brought to great heat with a view to cause evaporation, and the deposit of a sugary sediment. When the juice is sufficiently boiled down, it is removed into a copper boiler, and from this it is conveyed into a shallow wooden vessel, in which it crystallizes. After the lapse of a few hours, the dark-looking mass, consisting of sugar and liquid molasses (*treacle*, being that part of the juice which will not crystallize), is put into hogsheads with holes bored in the bottom. These hogsheads are set on wooden frames over a tank, into which the treacle drains, after which the hogsheads are filled up, headed in, and are ready for exportation.

XXVI. DAYBREAK.

See, the day begins to break,
And the light shoots like a streak
Of subtle fire ; the wind blows cold,
While the morning doth unfold.
Now the birds begin to rouse,
And the squirrel from the boughs
Leaps, to get him nuts and fruit;
The early lark, that erst was mute,
Carols to the rising day
Many a note and many a lay.

FLETCHER.

XXVII. SPENSER.

Edmund Spenser is an English poet of great note. He was born in 1553, about a hundred and fifty-three years after the death of Chaucer, and London was his birthplace also. The English language had greatly advanced since the time of Chaucer ; it was rich in poems of different kinds, and in ballads sung by the people. The poems of Spenser may be read with little difficulty, very few obsolete words occurring in them. His language is very fine, and his verses are very sweet. The *Fairy Queen* is his longest and finest poem. It is an allegory, in which virtues and vices are described as knights and ladies, and the struggles of the human heart are pictured forth in battles and adventures. Una and the lion, in the first book of the *Fairy Queen*, are well known, often seen in pictures and alluded to in books. The lady lost in the desert, and the lion, overcome by her beauty and goodness, guiding and protecting her, are described in verses that have become famous. Spenser was a scholar, bred at Cambridge, and a friend of many of the great men of his day. Queen Elizabeth gave him a pension and a post in Ireland. But in an insurrection that broke out there, his house was set on fire, his infant child perished in the flames, and all his property was lost. These misfortunes affected him so deeply, that he died three months afterwards, in 1599. He was buried in Westminster Abbey, near Chaucer.

XXVIII. THE CROW AND THE PITCHER.

A crow, ready to die with thirst, flew with joy to a pitcher which he saw at a distance. But when he came up to it, he found the water so low, that with all his stooping and straining he was unable to reach it. Thereupon he attempted to break the pitcher, then to overturn it; but his strength was not sufficient to do either. At last, seeing some small pebbles at hand, he dropped a great many of them into the pitcher, one by one, and so raised the water to the brim, and quenched his thirst.

Skill and patience will succeed where force fails. Necessity is the mother of invention.

XXIX. DEATH THE LEVELLER.

The glories of our birth and state
  Are shadows, not substantial things
There is no armour against fate,
  Death lays his icy hand on kings—
    Sceptre and crown
    Must tumble down,
And in the dust be equal made
With the poor crooked scythe and spade.
    All heads must come
    To the cold tomb;
Only the actions of the just
Smell sweet, and blossom in the dust.—SHIRLEY.

XXX. GREAT BRITAIN.

Yet unless I greatly deceive myself, the general effect of this checkered narrative will be to excite thankfulness in all religious minds, and hope in the breasts of all patriots. For the history of our country during the last hundred and sixty years, is eminently the history of physical, moral, and intellectual improvement. Those who compare the age on which their lot has fallen with a golden age which exists only in their imagination, may talk of degeneracy and decay; but no man who is correctly informed as to the past, will be disposed to take a morose or desponding view of the present.—MACAULAY's *History of England.*

XXXI. THE WOLF AND THE SHEPHERDS.

A wolf, looking into a hut, and seeing some shepherds comfortably regaling themselves on a joint of mutton: "A pretty row," said he, "these men would have made had they caught me at such a supper!"

Men are too apt to condemn in others the very things that they practise themselves.

XXXII. WHAT IS TAPIOCA?

The Mandioca or Tapioca used in South America is derived from a large root which grows wild, and is also cultivated in large quantities. The plant when growing is very poisonous, but its roots, when ripe, and after they have been exposed to the heat of the fire, are quite harmless. The natives first wash the roots, and then grate them upon a wooden rasp into cold water. The water being poured off, a starchy sediment remains at the bottom of the vessel, and this is dried over a slow fire and prepared afterwards for food. It is often used for puddings in England, and is considered light and nourishing.

XXXIII. "THE SHIP AT ANCHOR."

A Tavern.

A sailor, who was in the habit of spending all his money at the public-house, one day made a vow to be temperate in future, and kept it. Meeting with an old friend about a twelvemonth afterwards, the following conversation took place:—

Peter. Hollo, Jack! here you are, back from America.

Jack. Yes, Master Peter.

Peter. Won't you come in, and have a glass this cold day?

Jack. No, Master Peter, no! I cannot drink.

Peter. What, Jack, can you pass the door of the "Ship at Anchor" without taking a cup with your friends?

Jack. Impossible, Master Peter. I have a swelling here; don't you see it?

Peter. Ah! that is because you don't drink your grog as you used to do. Drink, my boy, and the swelling will soon go down.

Jack. You are quite right there! [*He pulls out of his pocket a large leathern purse full of money.*] There's the swelling I have given myself by steering clear of the "Ship at Anchor." If I begin drinking again, it will soon go down; there is not the least doubt of that.

Peter. Is it possible you have saved so much money, Jack?

Jack. It is, indeed, and I mean to go on doing it; and when I pass the "Ship at Anchor" after my next voyage, I hope to show you a new swelling on the other side.

XXXIV. WHAT IS FLAX?

Flax is grown in Great Britain, especially in Ireland, but also, to a large extent, in France, Holland, Germany, Italy, Egypt, and India. It has always been of great importance to the human race. The stalk is long and slender, branching at the top, and bearing several beautiful light-blue flowers, about the size of a large buttercup. These are succeeded by little round pods of seed, each about as large as a garden-pea, and containing several of the little flat brown seeds called *linseed*, from which we extract oil. The stalk is not more than half as thick as a wheaten straw, but very strong, because of the tough fibres which run through it from bottom to top. These fibres, when separated from the pith which is mixed with them, and the skin which covers them, are the flax from which linen is made. In order to obtain them, the plants are pulled up as soon as they have done flowering, and dried in the sun. Small bundles of them are then placed in the shallow part of a river or pond, stones or pieces of wood being laid on them to prevent their floating away. At other times they are simply exposed to the night dew. The moisture which they thus imbibe, quickly causes the soft skin which covers the fibres to decay.

After this process is completed, the bundles are spread out to dry, and when dried, the whole stalk can be easily rubbed to a powder, with the exception of the fibres, which are not impaired by the process. The bundles of fibres are next beaten with a heavy wooden implement, or *scutched*, as it is called ; and to remove the skin and pith broken up by this process, they are next heckled, or drawn through a peculiar kind of iron comb. The fibres which remain after these two operations are raw flax, and are fine enough for making coarse linen cloths ; but they require to be heckled over and over again, through much finer combs, to render them suitable for the manufacturing of fine linen, lawn, and lace.

XXXV. THE ASS'S SHADOW.

A youth, one hot summer's day, hired an ass to carry him from Athens to Megara. At mid-day the heat of the sun was so scorching that he dismounted, and would have sat down to repose himself under the shadow of the ass. But the driver of the ass disputed the place with him, declaring that he had an equal right to it.

"What!" said the youth; "did I not hire the ass for the whole journey?"

"Yes," said the other, "you hired the ass, but not the ass's shadow."

While they were thus wrangling and fighting for the place, the ass took to his heels and ran away.

XXXVI. CHILDE HAROLD'S GOOD-NIGHT.

Adieu, adieu! my native shore
 Fades o'er the waters blue;
The night-winds sigh, the breakers roar,
 And shrieks the wild sea-mew.
Yon sun that sets upon the sea
 We follow in his flight;
Farewell a while to him and thee:
 My native land—Good-night!

BYRON.

XXXVII. WHAT IS HEMP?

The Hemp plant goes through a similar process to the Flax, but is much coarser, and grows to a height of more than six feet. Great quantities are produced in Russia and Poland, and also, though not to the same extent, in Prussia, Germany, Austria, Italy, India, and the United States of America. It would be hard to say what we should do without this very useful plant, for, from the fibres of its stem, after they have been separated and cleaned by processes similar to those described in the case of flax, we make cloth for the sails of our ships, and ropes for their rigging; and although many substitutes have been proposed for it, none has been found to answer so well. In addition to sail-cloth and cordage, finer cloths and string of all kinds are made from it.

XXXVIII. WHAT IS COTTON?

Cotton consists of the fine long hairs which grow from the seeds of several varieties of *Gossypium*. These hairs are so long and numerous, that they completely fill the pod or seed-vessel. They are very delicate, of the same size throughout, but seldom jointed, and they are each separate from the other. The cotton-plant is chiefly cultivated in the Southern States of North America and in India. It is produced in great abundance, and is exported to England, where it is manufactured into cloth. The cotton factories are chiefly in Lancashire.

XXXIX. THE TWO OXFORD STUDENTS.

Leopold. John, go to Mr. Marcus's room, and ask him to lend me Livingstone's *Travels in Africa.*

John. Mr. Marcus, my master sends me to beg you will lend him Livingstone's *Travels.*

Marcus. Tell Mr. Leopold that I make it a rule never to lend my books, but if he will take the trouble to come to my room, he can read Livingstone's *Travels* as long as he likes.

Three months after.

Marcus. Thomas, go and ask Mr. Leopold to lend me his bellows to blow my fire. You will never be able to light it without them, I am quite sure.

Thomas. Mr. Leopold, your friend Mr. Marcus has sent me to beg the loan of your bellows to blow his fire.

Leopold. I am very sorry. Give my compliments to Mr. Marcus, and tell him I make it a rule never to lend my bellows; but if he will give himself the trouble of coming into my room, he is welcome to blow my fire as long as he likes.

XL. SHAKSPEARE.

William Shakspeare would come first on our list of great poets were we placing them according to merit, instead of years. He is allowed to be the greatest poet the world has ever seen, and his works have influenced the literature and thought of England, and do still influence it, more than the writings of any other man. Of his personal history we know very little, though many attempts have been made to twist surmises into facts. He was born at Stratford, on the river Avon, in Warwickshire, April 23, 1564, and he died there on the same day of the month, 1616. The greater part of his life was spent in London, where he was the friend and companion of all the great men of the time, and a favourite with Queen Elizabeth and James I. His occupation was that of an actor. Most of his works are written for the stage, and consist of historical dramas, of tragedies and comedies. It would be difficult to single out of these any better than the rest, so fine are the characters from the highest to the lowest, so suited to each are the speeches given them to utter. Any one wishing to have the richest library attainable in the smallest number of volumes, to become acquainted with the purest and best English, to study the highest standards of beauty in character and sentiment, should purchase Shakspeare's works, and read and re-read them till they become to him familiar friends. The Englishman who does not know and read Shakspeare, does not know one of England's greatest glories, and will never be able to estimate fully all that his country's language can express.

XLI. THE ASS AND THE LAMB.

" How hard is my fate !
What sorrows await,"
Said the Ass to the Sheep, " my deplorable state !

Cold, naked, ill-fed,
I sleep in a shed,
Where the snow wind, and rain come in over my head.

All this day did I pass
In a yard without grass :
What a pity that I was created an Ass !

As for master,—he sat
By the fire, with the Cat ;
And they both look, as you do, contented and fat.

Your nice coat of wool,
So elastic and full,
Makes you much to be envied,—ay, more than the bull."

" How can you pretend,"
Said her poor bleating friend,
" To complain ? Let me silence to you recommend.

My sorrows are deep,"
Continued the Sheep,
And her eyes look'd as if she were ready to weep.

" I expect,—'tis no fable,—
To be dragged from the stable,
And, to-morrow, perhaps, cut up for the table.

Now you—with docility,
Strength, and civility,—
Will live some years longer in all probability.

So no envy, I beg,
For I'll bet you an egg,
You will carry the spinach to eat with my leg."

MORAL.

The situation of those we envy is often much worse than our own.

XLII. CORAL.

Coral is a secretion from the body of an animal, very low in the scale of creation, called a polyp. The secretion forms a kind of outer skeleton or house for the little animal. Every fresh set of polyps builds on the top of the preceding, and thus, in the course of time, are constructed those coral reefs, which ultimately become habitable islands. Coral is a beautiful and curious material, highly prized for ornaments, especially when of a red or black colour. The little coral polyps inhabit chiefly the Mediterranean Sea, the Persian Gulf, the Red Sea, and the Indian Ocean.

XLIII. IVORY.

Ivory is the substance of the large tusks of the elephant, which grow out from either side of the mouth, somewhat like horns. It is much valued for its whiteness, fine grain, and the good polish that it takes. In the countries where elephants abound, hunting them for their tusks is a very profitable though perilous and laborious employment. Our supply of this article comes chiefly from Africa, India, Ceylon, and the countries north of the Malay Peninsula.

XLIV. THE GOOD LIFE A LONG LIFE.

It is not growing like a tree
In bulk, doth make man better be;
Or standing long—an oak three hundred year—
To fall a log at last, dry, bald, and sere.
A lily of a day
Is fairer far in May,
Although it fall and die that night:
It was the plant and flower of light.
In small proportions we just beauties see,
And in short measures life may perfect be.

BEN JONSON.

XLV. POTTERY.

Pottery is one of the most ancient as well as one of the most interesting of the arts. From its simplicity it has probably been one of the first manufactures of every nation, sun-dried bricks being one of its earliest products. The chief substance used by the potter is the well-known material *clay*. Alumina (the oxide of the metal aluminum) united with silica or sand, forms what may be called a typical clay. But most clays contain in addition lime, magnesia, potash, oxide of iron, and other ingredients. Clays which contain little or no oxide of iron are either naturally white or they burn white in the kiln. Such clays are rare, and are highly prized for the finer kinds of pottery.

Bricks, tiles, drain-pipes, and common brown earthenware vessels, as basins, cans, flower-pots, and the like, are made of ordinary clay, which always burns red in consequence of the presence of iron in its composition.

XLVI. POTTERY—*continued*.

For the white ware of our tables the finer clays of Cornwall, Devonshire, and Dorsetshire are alone used; the beautiful china clay from the decomposing granites of Cornwall being the chief ingredient in English china or porcelain. A similar material has been in use for centuries in making the famous Chinese porcelain; but it has been known in Europe only since the beginning of the eighteenth century. Potters' clay is always mixed with a certain proportion of ground flints, and great care and labour are bestowed upon its preparation. Grinding-mills and sieves of various kinds are used to free it from lumps, and to bring it to a fine general consistency resembling dough. The prepared clay is called the *body* or *paste*, and is afterwards either "thrown" on a wheel, or "pressed" into moulds which give it the desired form.

XLVII. THE DOCTOR'S SERVANT.

She was about thirty years old, and had a sufficiently plump and cheerful face, though it was twisted up into an odd expression of tightness that made it comical. But the extraordinary homeliness of her gait and manner would have superseded any face in the world. To say that she had two left legs and somebody else's arms, and that all four limbs seemed to be out of joint, and to start from perfectly wrong places when they were set in motion, is to offer the mildest outline of the reality. To say that she was perfectly content and satisfied with these arrangements, and regarded them as being no business of hers, and took her arms and legs as they came, and allowed them to dispose of themselves just as it happened, is to render faint justice to her equanimity.

XLVIII. THE DOCTOR'S SERVANT—*continued*.

Her dress was a prodigious pair of self-willed shoes, that never wanted to go where her feet went; blue stockings; a printed gown of many colours, and the most hideous pattern procurable for money; and a white apron. She always wore short sleeves, and always had by some accident grazed elbows, in which she took so lively an interest that she was continually trying to turn them round and get impossible views of them. In general, a little cap perched somewhere on her head, though it was rarely to be met with in the place usually occupied in other subjects by that article of dress; but from head to foot she was scrupulously clean, and maintained a kind of dislocated tidiness. Indeed, her laudable anxiety to be tidy and compact in her own conscience as well as in the public eyes, gave rise to one of her most startling evolutions, which was to grasp herself sometimes by a sort of wooden handle (part of her clothing, and familiarly called a busk), and wrestle, as it were, with her garments, until they fell into a symmetrical arrangement.
DICKENS.

XLIX. NATURE.

It is more accurate to avoid the usual classification of objects in nature into Animal, Vegetable, and Mineral, and to regard them as divided into two kingdoms, the ORGANIC and the INORGANIC.

Everything that has life, whether it be animal or vegetable, is made up of one or more organs, by means of which the processes of life, such as circulation and digestion, are carried on. Things destitute of life, on the contrary, have need of none of these organs, whether they be tubes, cells, or vessels for the continuance of their existence, and they are therefore called Inorganic. Of inorganic things, we may say that all those which are either metallic or earthy are minerals, or belong to the Mineral Kingdom.
J. BEETE JUKES.

L. THE BALD KNIGHT.

A certain knight growing old, his hair fell off, and he became bald, to hide which imperfection he wore a periwig. But as he was riding out with some others hunting, a sudden gust of wind blew off the periwig, and exposed his bald pate. The company could not forbear laughing at the accident; and he himself laughed louder than anybody, saying: "How was it to be expected that I should keep strange hair upon my head, when my own would not stay there?"

LI. MILTON.

John Milton was born in London in 1608. He was therefore eight years of age when Shakspeare died. His name stands next to that of Shakspeare as England's second greatest poet, and his chief fame rests on his poem of Paradise Lost. This famous work describes the happiness of man in Eden, his fall and banishment. It is full of grand imagery and vigorous thought, and was written after the poet became blind. Some of his shorter poems —the Hymn to the Nativity, written at college, Comus, Lycidas, and his Sonnets—are among the finest in the language.

Milton was carefully educated, and was a Cambridge student. He lived during a time of civil war, and sided with the Puritans, so that some of his poems bear traces of their peculiar views. His domestic life was not a happy one, and he was blind for twenty-two years. He died in 1674.

LII. FROM PARADISE LOST, BOOK V.

So spake the Seraph Abdiel, faithful found
Among the faithless,—faithful only he
Among innumerable false; unmoved,
Unshaken, unseduced, unterrified,
His loyalty he kept, his love, his zeal;

Nor number nor example with him wrought
To swerve from truth or change his constant mind
Though single. From amidst them forth he passed,
Long way through hostile scorn, which he sustained
Superior, nor of violence feared aught;
And, with retorted scorn, his back he turned
On those proud towers to swift destruction doomed.

MILTON.

LIII. "A SOFT ANSWER TURNETH AWAY WRATH."

The horse of a pious man in Massachusetts happening to stray into the road, a neighbour of the man who owned the horse put him in the pound. Meeting the owner soon after, he told him what he had done, and added, "If I ever catch him in the road hereafter, I'll do just so again."

"Neighbour," replied the other, "not long since I looked out of my window in the night, and saw your cattle in my mowing-ground, and I drove them out and shut them in your yard : *I'll do it again.*" Struck with the reply, the man liberated the horse from the pound, and paid the charges himself.

LIV. DRYDEN.

John Dryden was born in 1631, when Milton was a young man twenty-three years of age, and he was forty-three years of age when the blind poet died. He too was educated at Cambridge. He published his first poem at the age of eighteen, and up to the last year of his life, at the age of sixty-eight, he was still giving to the world his brilliant rhymes ; his last poems being among the best he ever wrote. His works comprise poems in almost every style ; but his satirical powers were greater than those of his fancy or imagination, hence it is as a satirist that he is most admired. His life was as changeful as the times in which he lived ; and he had often to write for his bread. He was buried in Westminster Abbey with public honours.

LV. CONTENTMENT.

There is a jewel which no Indian mine can buy,
No chemic art can counterfeit:
It makes men rich in greatest poverty;
Makes water wine, turns wooden cups to gold,
The homely whistle to sweet music's strain:
Seldom it comes, to few from heaven sent—
That much in little, all in naught—CONTENT.

LVI. MINES AND MINERALS.

A large amount of our comforts and wealth is due to the minerals which the skill of man procures out of the bowels of the earth. The export and import of various minerals form a leading feature of the commerce of the globe, employing and enriching alike the inhabitants of those countries which send away and those which receive them. Of iron alone, about a million tons are annually exported from Britain, while she in turn imports several million ounces of gold. The procuring of the various minerals, and the manufacturing of them into articles of use, such as machinery from iron, water-pipes from lead, boilers and other vessels from copper, culinary utensils from tin and its alloys, and watches and ornaments from silver and gold, afford occupation to thousands of our fellow-men, and give a field for the exercise of ingenuity and invention to those who work in them.

The various materials obtained through the operations of the miner occur either in parallel layers called *strata* or *seams*, or they penetrate the rents and fissures of rocks, and form what are called *veins* or *lodes*. Of the former, coal, limestone, and clay iron-ore are examples; and of the latter, the ores of lead, copper, tin, zinc, and of most of the metals. Of course the mode of mining a seam and a vein must so far differ; but as all the modes of operation more or less resemble each other, it will be sufficient to describe the manner of obtaining coal, one of the most useful and familiar of our minerals.

LVII. THE TWO SPRINGS.

Two springs, which issued from the same mountain, began their course together: one of them took her way in a silent and gentle stream, while the other rushed along with a sounding and rapid current. "Sister," said the latter, "at the rate you move, you will probably be dried up before you advance much farther; whereas, for myself, I will venture a wager, that, within two or three hundred furlongs, I shall become navigable; and, after distributing commerce and wealth wherever I flow, I shall majestically proceed to pay my tribute to the ocean. So, farewell, dear sister! and patiently submit to your fate."

Her sister made no reply; but, calmly descending to the meadows below, increased her stream, by numberless little rills, which she collected in her progress, till, at length, she was enabled to rise into a considerable river; whilst the proud stream, who had the vanity to depend solely upon her own sufficiency, continued a shallow brook; and was glad, at last, to be helped forward, by throwing herself into the arms of her despised sister.

MORAL.

His strength in words the blusterer vainly spends,
While steadiness in quiet gains its ends.

FROM DODSLEY.

LVIII. POPE.

Alexander Pope was born in 1688. He was therefore eleven years of age when Dryden died, but delighted to recall the fact that he had seen that famous poet. He began to write as a boy of sixteen, and died in the height of his fame at the age of fifty-six. He wrote a great deal of satire; but his verses are highly polished, his language elegant and full of point. Many of his lines are familiar to us as proverbs. His Essay on Man is his most admired work. He died in 1744.

LIX. KNOWLEDGE.

Fired at first sight with what the muse imparts,
In fearless youth we tempt the height of arts;
While from the bounded level of our mind
Short views we take, nor see the lengths behind:
But, more advanced, behold with strange surprise,
New distant scenes of endless science rise.
So, pleased at first, the towering Alps we try,
Mount o'er the vales and seem to tread the sky;
The eternal snows appear already past,
And the first clouds and mountains seem the last.
But, those attained, we tremble to survey
The growing labours of the lengthen'd way;
The increasing prospect tires our wand'ring eyes,
Hills peep o'er hills and Alps on Alps arise.

POPE.

LX. ON IRON.

Iron greatly excels all other metals in importance. The more closely we study its employment in the arts, the more we wonder at and admire its multitudinous and widely different uses. We see it in the ponderous fly-wheel of the steam-engine, amounting sometimes to a mass of many tons, and can trace it through a million gradations of smaller objects, in all of which it scarcely admits of a substitute, till we come to the most delicate watch-spring. Often, too, it admirably replaces other materials, as timber or stone, with the advantages of greater strength, or lightness, or beauty, as in the Leviathan steam-ship, the Menai Bridge, and the Crystal Palace. Iron is also extensively employed in the manufacture of ink, dyes, and pigments; and in medicine as well as in photography. But, before we dwell longer on the manifold uses of this most interesting metal, we must look at the mode in which it is extracted from its ores, and converted into Cast Iron, Malleable Iron, and Steel.

LXI. WORDSWORTH.

William Wordsworth was born in 1770. There is an interval, therefore, of twenty-six years between his birth and the death of Pope. But England had many poets in that interval, and among them Goldsmith, Burns, and Cowper stand pre-eminent. These poets had paved the way for Wordsworth's writings, for they had left the polished and artificial style of Pope for more simple and natural verses. Of Burns this is especially true. He was a Scotch peasant, and his poems are songs and ballads more like those alluded to as belonging to the early epoch of English poetry. In those days verses like these were all the people had of literature, and they handed them down from parent to child, household possessions, exquisite for their simplicity and pathos. Of this natural school Wordsworth is the great master.

Wordsworth's poems are of country life and simple people; he is pathetic and tender, and when he describes a scene in nature he does it so that every detail is present to the reader's eye as it was to the poet's. He wrote many years before his genius was recognised, but he is now so popular that his poems are to be found in every collection. He died at the age of eighty in 1850, and is buried among the Westmoreland hills and lakes of which he sang.

Many poets lived and wrote during his long life. Byron, Shelley, Keats, Coleridge, Southey, and Scott, may be named. Wordsworth was poet-laureate, an honour since conferred on our greatest living poet, Alfred Tennyson, whose verses on the charge at Balaclava are or should be known to every English boy.

LXII. A WELCOME TO PRINCESS ALEXANDRA.
By the Poet Laureate.

Sea-kings' daughter from over the sea,
       Alexandra!
Saxon and Norman and Dane are we,
But all of us Danes in our welcome of thee,
       Alexandra!

Welcome her, thunders of fort and of fleet!
Welcome her, thundering cheer of the street!
Welcome her, all things youthful and sweet,
Scatter the blossom under her feet!
Break, happy land, into earlier flowers!
Make music, O bird, in the new-budded bowers!
Welcome her, welcome her, all that is ours!
Warble, O bugle, and trumpet blare!
Flags, flutter out upon turrets and towers!
Flames, on the windy headland flare!
Utter your jubilee, steeple and spire!
Clash, ye bells, in the merry March air!
Flash, ye cities, in rivers of fire!
Welcome her, welcome the land's desire,
       Alexandra!
Sea-kings' daughter as happy as fair,
Blissful bride of a blissful heir,
Bride of the heir of the kings of the sea,
O joy to the people and joy to the throne,
Come to us, love us, and make us your own:
For Saxon or Dane or Norman we,
Teuton or Celt, or whatever we be,
We are each all Dane in our welcome of thee,
       Alexandra!
         TENNYSON.

LXIII. LOVEGOLD AND JAMES.—(*Fielding.*)

[*Lovegold* alone. Enter *James.*]

Lovegold. Where have you been? I have wanted you above an hour.

James. Whom do you want, sir, your coachman or your cook? for I am both one and the other.

Love. I want my cook.

James. I thought, indeed, it was not your coachman; for you have had no great occasion for him since your last pair of horses were starved; but your cook, sir, shall wait upon you in an instant. [*Puts off his coachman's greatcoat, and appears as a cook.*] Now, sir, I am ready for your commands.

Love. I am engaged this evening to give a supper.

James. A *supper*, sir! I have not heard the word this half-year; a dinner, indeed, now and then; but for a *supper*, I am almost afraid, for want of practice,—my hand is out.

Love. Leave off your saucy jesting, and see that you provide a good supper.

James. That may be done with a great deal of money, sir.

Love. Is the mischief in you? always money! Can you say nothing else but *money, money, money?* My children, my servants, my relatives, can pronounce nothing but *money.*

James. Well, sir; but how many will there be at the table?

Love. About eight or ten; but I will have a supper dressed but for eight; for, if there be enough for eight, there is enough for ten.

James. Suppose, sir, at one end, a handsome soup; at the other, a fine Westphalia ham and chickens; on the one side, a fillet of veal; on the other, a turkey, or rather a bustard, which may be had for about a guinea—

Love. What! is the fellow providing an entertainment for my lord mayor and the court of aldermen?

James. Then a RAGOUT—

Love. I'll have no ragout. Would you burst the good people?

James. Then pray, sir, what *will* you have?

Love. Why, see and provide something to cloy their stomachs; let there be two good dishes of soup-maigre; a large suet pudding; some dainty fat pork-pie, *very* fat;

a fine small lean breast of mutton; and a large dish with two artichokes. There; that's plenty and variety.

James. Oh dear—

Love. Plenty and variety.

James. But, sir, you must have some poultry.

Love. No; I'll have none.

James. Indeed, sir, you should.

Love. Well, then, kill the old hen; for she has done laying.

James. Mercy! sir, how the folks will talk of it; indeed, people say enough of you already.

Love. Eh! why, what do the people say, pray?

James. Ah, sir, if I could be assured you would not be angry.

Love. Not at all; for I am always glad to hear what the world says of me.

James. Why, sir, since you *will* have it then, they make a jest of you everywhere; nay, of your servants on your account. One says you pick a quarrel with them quarterly, in order to find an excuse to pay them no wages.

Love. Pooh! pooh!

James. Another says you were taken one night stealing your own oats from your own horses.

Love. That must be a lie; for I never allow them any.

James. In a word, you are the by-word everywhere; and you are never mentioned, but by the names of covetous, stingy, scraping, old—

Love. Get along, you impudent villain!

James. Nay, sir, you said you would not be angry.

Love. Get out, you dog! you—

LXIV. ON ADDISON.

When this man, Addison, looks from the world, whose weaknesses he describes so benevolently, up to the Heaven which shines over us all, I can hardly fancy a human face lighted up with a more serene rapture; a human intellect thrilling with a purer love and adoration than

Joseph Addison. Listen to him: from your childhood you have known the verses; but who can hear their sacred music without love and awe?

> "Soon as the evening shades prevail,
> The moon takes up the wondrous tale,
> And, nightly to the listening earth,
> Repeats the story of her birth;
> While all the stars that round her burn,
> And all the planets in their turn,
> Confirm the tidings as they roll,
> And spread the truth from pole to pole.
>
> "What though in solemn silence all
> Move round the dark terrestrial ball?
> What though no real voice or sound
> Amidst their radiant orbs be found?
> In reason's ear they all rejoice,
> And utter forth a glorious voice;
> For ever singing, as they shine,
> 'The hand that made us is divine.'"

It seems to me those verses shine like the stars. They shine out of a great deep calm. When he turns to Heaven, a Sabbath comes over that man's mind; and his face lights up from it with a glory of thanks and prayer. His sense of religion stirs through his whole being. In the fields, in the town; looking at the birds in the trees; at the children in the streets; in the morning or in the moonlight; over his books in his own room; in a happy party at a country merry-making, or a town assembly, goodwill and peace to God's creatures, and love and awe of Him who made them, fill his pure heart and shine from his kind face. If Swift's life was the most wretched, I think Addison's was one of the most enviable. A life prosperous and beautiful; a calm death; an immense fame and affection afterwards for his happy and spotless name.

THACKERAY'S *English Humorists.*

LXV. TRAVELLING IN ENGLAND IN THE SEVENTEENTH CENTURY.

Of all inventions, the alphabet and the printing-press alone excepted, those inventions which abridge distance have done most for the civilisation of our species. Every improvement of the means of locomotion benefits mankind morally and intellectually as well as materially, and not only facilitates the interchange of the various productions of nature and art, but tends to remove national and provincial antipathies, and to bind together all the branches of the great human family. In the seventeenth century the inhabitants of London were, for almost every practical purpose, farther from Reading than they now are from Edinburgh, and farther from Edinburgh than they now are from Vienna.

The subjects of Charles the Second were not, it is true, quite unacquainted with that principle which has, in our own time, produced an unprecedented revolution in human affairs, which has enabled navies to advance in the face of wind and tide, and battalions, attended by all their baggage and artillery, to traverse kingdoms at a pace equal to that of the fleetest race-horse. The Marquis of Worcester had recently observed the expansive power of moisture rarefied by heat. After many experiments he had succeeded in constructing a rude steam-engine, which he called a fire water work, and which he pronounced to be an admirable and most forcible instrument of propulsion. But the Marquis was suspected to be a madman, and known to be a Papist. His inventions, therefore, found no favourable reception. His fire water work might, perhaps, furnish matter for conversation at a meeting of the Royal Society, but was not applied to any practical purpose. There were no railways, except a few made of timber, from the mouths of the Northumbrian coal pits to the banks of the Tyne.

There was very little internal communication by water. A few attempts had been made to deepen and embank the natural streams, but with slender success. Hardly a single navigable canal had been even projected. The English of that day were in the habit of talking with mingled admiration and despair of the immense trench, by which Louis the Fourteenth had made a junction between the Atlantic and the Mediterranean. They little thought that their country would, in the course of a few generations, be intersected, at the cost of private adventurers, by artificial rivers making up more than four times the length of the Thames, the Severn, and the Trent together.

It was by the highways that both travellers and goods generally passed from place to place. And those highways appear to have been far worse than might have been expected from the degree of wealth and civilisation which the nation had even then attained. On the best lines of communication the ruts were deep, the descents precipitous, and the way often such as it was hardly possible to distinguish, in the dusk, from the unenclosed heath and fen which lay on both sides.

It was only in fine weather that the whole breadth of the road was available for wheeled vehicles. Often the mud lay deep on the right and the left; and only a narrow track of firm ground rose above the quagmire. At such times obstructions and quarrels were frequent, and the path was sometimes blocked up during a long time by carriers, neither of whom would break the way. It happened, almost every day, that coaches stuck fast, until a team of cattle could be procured from some neighbouring farm to tug them out of the slough. But in bad seasons the traveller had to encounter inconveniences still more serious. Thoresby, who was in the habit of travelling between Leeds and the capital, has recorded, in his Diary, such a series of perils and disasters as might suffice for a journey to the Frozen Ocean or to the Desert of Sahara.

On one occasion he learned that the floods were out between Ware and London, that passengers had to swim for their lives, and that a higgler had perished in the attempt to cross. In consequence of these tidings he turned out of the high road, and was conducted across some meadows, where it was necessary for him to ride to the saddle-skirts in water.

In the course of another journey he narrowly escaped being swept away by an inundation of the Trent. He was afterwards detained at Stamford four days on account of the state of the roads, and then ventured to proceed only because fourteen members of the House of Commons, who were going up in a body to Parliament with guides and numerous attendants, took him into their company. On the roads of Derbyshire travellers were in constant fear for their necks, and were frequently compelled to alight and lead their beasts. The great route through Wales to Holyhead was in such a state that, in 1685, a viceroy, going to Ireland, was five hours in travelling fourteen miles, from Saint Asaph to Conway. Between Conway and Beaumaris he was forced to walk great part of the way; and his lady was carried in a litter. His coach was, with great difficulty, and by the help of many hands, brought after him entire. In general, carriages were taken to pieces at Conway, and borne, on the shoulders of stout Welsh peasants, to the Menai Straits.

In some parts of Kent and Sussex none but the strongest horses could, in winter, get through the bog, in which, at every step, they sank deep. The markets were often inaccessible during several months. It is said that the fruits of the earth were sometimes suffered to rot in one place, while in another place, distant only a few miles, the supply fell far short of the demand. The wheeled carriages were, in this district, generally pulled by oxen. When

Prince George of Denmark visited the stately mansion of Petworth in wet weather, he was six hours in going nine miles; and it was necessary that a body of sturdy hinds should be on each side of his coach in order to prop it. Of the carriages which conveyed his retinue several were upset and injured. A letter from one of his gentlemen-in-waiting has been preserved, in which the unfortunate courtier complains that, during fourteen hours, he never once alighted, except when his coach was overturned or stuck fast in the mud.

On the best highways heavy articles were, in the time of Charles the Second, generally conveyed from place to place by stage waggons. In the straw of these vehicles nestled a crowd of passengers, who could not afford to travel by coach or on horseback, and who were prevented by infirmity, or by the weight of their luggage, from going on foot. The expense of transmitting heavy goods in this way was enormous. From London to Birmingham the charge was seven pounds a ton; from London to Exeter twelve pounds a ton. This was about fifteen pence a ton for every mile, more by a third than was afterwards charged on turnpike roads, and fifteen times what is now demanded by railway companies. The cost of conveyance amounted to a prohibitory tax on many useful articles. Coal, in particular, was never seen except in the districts where it was produced, or in the districts to which it could be carried by sea, and was indeed always known in the south of England by the name of sea-coal.

MACAULAY.

LXVI. THE BETTER LAND.

"I hear thee speak of the better land;
Thou callest its children a happy band:
Mother! O where is that radiant shore?—
Shall we not seek it, and weep no more?—

Is it where the flower of the orange blows,
And the fire-flies dance through the myrtle boughs?"
"Not there, not there, my child!"

"Is it where the feathery palm-trees rise,
And the date grows ripe under sunny skies?—
Or 'midst the green islands on glittering seas,
Where fragrant forests perfume the breeze,
And strange bright birds, on their starry wings,
Bear the rich hues of all glorious things?"
"Not there, not there, my child!"

"Is it far away in some region old,
Where the rivers wander o'er sands of gold?
Where the burning rays of the ruby shine,
And the diamond lights up the secret mine,
And the pearl gleams forth from the coral strand,
Is it there, sweet mother, that better land?"
"Not there, not there, my child!—

"Eye hath not seen it, my gentle boy!
Ear hath not heard its deep songs of joy;
Dreams cannot picture a world so fair—
Sorrow and death may not enter there:
Time doth not breathe on its fadeless bloom;
For beyond the clouds, and beyond the tomb,
It is there, it is there, my child!"

MRS. HEMANS.

LXVII. WONDERS OF CIVILISATION.

The condition of the present inhabitants of this country is very different from that of their forefathers. These, generally divided into small states or societies, had few relations of amity with surrounding tribes, and their thoughts and interests were confined very much within their own little territories and rude habits. Now, however, every one sees himself a member of one vast civilized society which covers the face of the earth, and no part of the earth is indifferent to him. In England, a man of small fortune may cast his regards around him, and say with truth and exultation: "I am lodged in a house that affords me conveniences and comforts which even a king could not command some centuries ago. There are ships crossing the seas in every direction, to bring what is useful to me from all parts of the earth. In China, men are gathering the tea-leaf for me; in America, they are planting cotton for me; in the West India Islands, they are preparing my sugar and my coffee; in Italy, they are feeding silk-worms for me; in Saxony, they are shearing the sheep to make me clothing; at home, powerful steam-engines are spinning and weaving for me, and making cutlery for me, and pumping the mines that minerals useful to me may be procured.

"My patrimony was small, yet I have carriages running day and night on all the roads to carry my correspondence; I have roads, and canals, and bridges, to bear the coal for my winter fire; nay, I have protecting fleets and armies around my happy country, to secure my enjoyments and repose. Then I have editors and printers who daily send me an account of what is going on throughout the world, among all these people who serve me; and in a corner of my house I have *books*, the miracle of all my possessions, more wonderful than the wishing-cap of the Arabian tales; for they transport me instantly, not only to all places, but to all times. By my books I can conjure up before me, to vivid existence, all the great and good men of antiquity; and for my individual satisfaction, I can make them act over again the most renowned of their exploits; the orators declaim for me; the historians recite; the poets sing; in a word, from the equator to the pole, and from the beginning of time until now, by my books I can be where I please."—This picture is not overcharged, and might be much extended; such being the miracle of God's goodness and providence, that each individual of the civilized millions that cover the earth may have nearly the same enjoyments as if he were the single lord of all. ARNOTT.

LXVIII. THE FIRST PARLIAMENT.

It was a great date for England, that of the First Parliament. There had been a Council of the great landholders, secular and ecclesiastic, from Anglo-Saxon times; and it is believed by some that the Commons were at least occasionally and to some extent represented in it. But it was during a civil war, which took place in the middle of the thirteenth century, marvellously like that which marked the middle of the seventeenth, being for law against arbitrary royal power, that the first parliaments, properly so called, were assembled. Matthew of Paris, in his *Chronicle*, first uses the *word* in reference to a council of the barons in 1246. At length, in December 1264, when that extraordinary man, Simon de Montfort, Earl of Leicester—a mediæval Cromwell—held the weak King Henry III. in his power, and was really the head of the State, a parliament was summoned, in which there should be two knights for each county, and two citizens for every borough; the first clear acknowledgment of the Commons' element in the State.

This parliament met on the 20th of January 1265, in that magnificent hall at Westminster[1] which still survives, so interesting a monument of many of the most memorable events of English history. The representatives of the Commons sat in the same place with their noble associates, probably at the bottom of the hall, little disposed to assert a controlling voice, not joining indeed in any vote, for we hear of no such thing at first, and far of course from having any adequate sense of the important results that were to flow from their appearing there that day. There, however, they were—an admitted Power, entitled to be consulted in all great national movements, and, above all, to have a say in the matter of taxation. The summer months saw Leicester overpowered, and himself and nearly all his associates slaughtered; many changes afterwards

---
[1] Fabyan's Chronicle, L 356.

took place in the constitutional system of the country; but the *Commons*, once allowed to play a part in these great councils, were never again left out. Strange that other European states of high civilisation and intelligence should be scarcely yet arrived at a principle of popular representation, which England, in comparative barbarism, realized for herself six centuries ago!—CHAMBERS'S *Book of Days.*

LXIX. BATTLE OF BANNOCKBURN.

Here must they pause; for, in advance
As far as one might pitch a lance,
The Monarch rode along the van,
The foe's approaching force to scan,
His line to marshal and to range,
And ranks to square, and fronts to change.
Alone he rode—from head to heel
Sheathed in his ready arms of steel;
Nor mounted yet on war-horse wight,
But, till more near the shock of fight,
Reining a palfrey low and light.
A diadem of gold was set
Above his bright steel bassinet,
And clasp'd within its glittering twine
Was seen the glove of Argentine;
Truncheon or leading staff he lacks,
Bearing, instead, a battle-axe.
He ranged his soldiers for the fight,
Accoutred thus, in open sight
Of either host.—Three bowshots far,
Paused the deep front of England's war,
And rested on their arms awhile,
To close and rank their warlike file,
And hold high council, if that night
Should view the strife, or dawning light.

O gay, yet fearful to behold,
Flashing with steel and rough with gold,

And bristled o'er with bills and spears,
With plumes and pennons waving fair,
Was that bright battle-front! for there
    Rode England's King and peers:
And who, that saw that monarch ride,
His kingdom battled by his side,
Could then his direful doom foretell!—
Fair was his seat in knightly selle,
And in his sprightly eye was set
Some spark of the Plantagenet.
Though light and wandering was his glance,
It flash'd at sight of shield and lance.
" Know'st thou," he said, " De Argentine,
Yon knight who marshals thus their line?"
" The tokens on his helmet tell
The Bruce, my Liege: I know him well."
" And shall the audacious traitor brave
The presence where our banners wave?"
" So please, my Liege," said Argentine,
" Were he but horsed on steed like mine,
To give him fair and knightly chance,
I would adventure forth my lance."
" In battle-day," the King replied,
" Nice tourney rules are set aside.
—Still must the rebel dare our wrath?
Set on him—sweep him from our path!"
And, at King Edward's signal, soon
Dash'd from the ranks Sir Henry Boune.

LXX. OLIVER GOLDSMITH.

Goldsmith might now be considered as a prosperous man. He had the means of living in comfort, and even in what to one who had so often slept in barns and on bulks must have been luxury. His fame was great and was constantly rising. He lived in what was intellectually far the best society of the kingdom; in a society in which no talent or accomplishment was wanting, and in which the art of conversation was cultivated with splendid success.

There probably were never four talkers more admirable in four different ways than Johnson, Burke, Beauclerk, and Garrick; and Goldsmith was on terms of intimacy with all the four. He aspired to share in their colloquial renown; but never was ambition more unfortunate. It may seem strange that a man who wrote with so much perspicuity, vivacity, and grace, should have been, whenever he took a part in conversation, an empty, noisy, blundering rattle. But on this point the evidence is overwhelming. So extraordinary was the contrast between Goldsmith's published works and the silly things which he said, that Horace Walpole described him as an inspired idiot. "Noll," said Garrick, "wrote like an angel, and talked like poor Poll." Chamier declared that it was a hard exercise of faith to believe that so foolish a chatterer could have really written the *Traveller*. Even Boswell could say with contemptuous compassion, that he liked very well to hear honest Goldsmith run on. " Yes, sir," said Johnson, " but he should not like to hear himself."

Minds differ as rivers differ. There are transparent and sparkling rivers from which it is delightful to drink as they flow; to such rivers the minds of such men as Burke and Johnson may be compared. But there are rivers of which the water when first drawn is turbid and noisome, but becomes pellucid as crystal and delicious to the taste if it be suffered to stand till it has deposited a sediment; and such a river is a type of the mind of Goldsmith. His first thoughts on every subject were confused even to absurdity, but they required only a little time to work themselves clear. When he wrote they had that time; and therefore his readers pronounced him a man of genius: but when he talked he talked nonsense, and made himself the laughing-stock of his hearers. He was painfully sensible of his inferiority in conversation; he felt every failure keenly; yet he had not sufficient judgment and self-command to hold his tongue. His animal spirits and vanity were always impelling him to try to do the one thing which he could not do. After every attempt he felt that he had exposed himself, and writhed with shame and vexation; yet the next moment he began again.

His associates seem to have regarded him with kindness, which, in spite of their admiration of his writings, was not unmixed with contempt. In truth, there was in his character much to love, but very little to respect. His heart was soft even to weakness; he was so generous, that he quite forgot to be just; he forgave injuries so readily, that he might be said to invite them, and was so liberal to beggars, that he had nothing left for his tailor and his butcher. He was vain, sensual, frivolous, profuse, improvident. One vice of a darker shade was imputed to him, envy. But there is not the least reason to believe that this bad passion, though it sometimes made him wince and utter fretful exclamations, ever impelled him to injure by wicked arts the reputation of any of his rivals. The truth probably is, that he was not more envious, but merely less prudent than his neighbours. His heart was on his lips. All those small jealousies, which are but too common among men of letters, but which a man of letters who is also a man of the world does his best to conceal, Goldsmith avowed with the simplicity of a child. When he was envious, instead of affecting indifference, instead of damning with faint praise, instead of doing injuries slily and in the dark, he told everybody that he was envious. "Do not, pray, do not talk of Johnson in such terms," he said to Boswell; "you harrow up my very soul." George Steevens and Cumberland were men far too cunning to say such a thing. They would have echoed the praises of the man whom they envied, and then have sent to the newspapers anonymous libels upon him. Both what was good and what was bad in Goldsmith's character was to his associates a perfect security that he would never commit such villany. He was neither ill-natured enough, nor long-headed enough, to be guilty of any malicious act which required contrivance and disguise.   MACAULAY.

LXXI. NINTH REPORT OF HER MAJESTY'S CIVIL SERVICE COMMISSIONERS.

We, Your Majesty's Civil Service Commissioners, humbly offer to Your Majesty our Ninth Annual Report. The total number of nominations notified to us since the commencement of our proceedings has been 25,612. During the four years up to the end of December 1859, the nominations numbered 9752; during the last four years they have amounted to 14,757; those for the year 1863 being 3605.

The situations to which these nominations refer may be divided into two classes, which it will be convenient to treat separately, viz.,—(1.) Superior situations, clerkships, etc. (2.) Inferior situations, such as that of out-door officer, letter-carrier, warder, etc.

Class I. Superior Situations,[1] Clerkships, etc.

The number of nominations disposed of in this class has been 1429, and the number of certificates granted 609. Of the appointments thus filled 253 had been made the subject of competition among 813 candidates, and 356 of absolute nomination.

The ratio of the number of competitors to the number of vacancies for which they competed has varied but slightly during the six years; the range being from 2·6 for each vacancy, which was the proportion in 1860, to 3·0 for each vacancy in 1862. The fluctuations have been—

Year	Ratio
1858,	2·8 per vacancy.
1859,	2·9 ,,
1860,	2·6 ,,
1861,	2·7 ,,
1862,	3·0 ,,
1863,	2·9 ,,

---

[1] Under this head are comprised appointments in the Diplomatic and Consular Services. Inspectorships of Schools (Ireland), Inspectorships of Factories, etc.

It is to be added that, of the 813 competitors examined 291 were found to be below the standard of attainment requisite for a pass examination; leaving the *bona fide* competition to be between 522 candidates for 278 places, or in the proportion of only 1·9 to each vacancy.

As a general rule, strict inquiries are not made as to the age, health, or character of any competitors except those who are successful in the competition. The number of competitors actually rejected on these grounds has been 15; of whom 4 proved to be disqualified in respect of age, 7 in respect of health, and 4 in respect of character.

The following Table gives further particulars regarding the competitions for this class of appointments which have taken place since 1858 :—

Year.	Number of Competitions.	Number of Situations competed for.	Number of Nominees.	Number of Nominees who			
				Did not proceed to examination, or were ineligible.	Were eligible and examined.		
					Total.	Unsuccessful.	Successful.
1858	122	230	745	98	647	455	192
1859	96	286	869*	153	1107	849	258
1860	79	235	680	83	597	402	195
1861	94	266	812	97	715	479	236
1862	118	289	994	130	864	600	264
1863	133	278	920	107	813	554	259
Total,	642	1584	5020*	668	4743	3339	1404
Average,	107	264	837	111	791	557	234

The total number of candidates nominated during the year 1863 for preliminary test examination was 633; of whom 82, for various reasons, were not examined. Of the 551 who were examined, 284 passed, and 267 were rejected; the proportion of rejections being just 48·5 per cent.

* Excluding 391 candidates at the open competition for writerships in the India Office.

Of 515 candidates who received absolute nominations, 356 have obtained certificates ; 122 failed to pass their examination ; 5 proved ineligible in point of age ; 4 were unable to satisfy us of their fitness in respect of health, and 3 in respect of character. In 25 cases the nomination was cancelled, or the candidate failed to appear.

The total number of candidates of this class rejected in 1863, on age, health, and character, was 27 ; viz., 9 on the ground of age, 11 on the ground of health, and 7 of character.

Under the head of knowledge and ability we have found, as in former years, that nearly all the rejections have been due to failure in the elementary subjects. Throughout the whole of our proceedings, during eight years and a half, only 183 candidates of this class have been rejected without having failed in orthography, handwriting, or arithmetic ; the total number of rejections having amounted to 2334.[1]

---

[1] The subjects common to the examinations for all kinds of Government offices are : good, that is to say, distinct and legible, handwriting, writing from dictation, the making of préces or abstracts, and arithmetic, including vulgar and decimal fractions. Detailed information can be obtained by addressing requests to the Secretary, Civil Service Commission, Dean's Yard, Westminster, London.

EXTRACTS FROM NEWSPAPERS.

I. THE RIFLE.

The rifle is now firmly established as the national weapon of England. In the long interval which has elapsed since the yew bow went out, and the "cloth-yard shaft" had to give way to the more deadly bullet, we have taken up with all kinds of martial instruments, as our friends or enemies invented them. Toledo made us rapiers, and Bayonne bayonets, Bilboa the small sword, and Oriental smitheries the sabre; and we have taught our teachers how to use their own inventions upon more than one crowning field. . . . But in the rifle we have discovered a weapon which once more calls into play all those qualities that made the bow an English arm. It asks for strength, it asks for endurance of fatigue; calm nerve and clear eye after ever so much marching and counter-marching, and that control of the will over the muscles, and the man over the machine, which sent many a goose-winged arrow quivering into the heart of roe-deer, or the breasts of the Frenchman at Poitiers and Cressy, "five hundred foot him fro." . . . We know enough now of rifle-shooting to be extremely well convinced that there are better rifles than the Enfield. But the piece has merits of its own; it is the regulation musket; and, accordingly, with the Enfield as its main reliance, the Volunteer force has made sharp-shooting an English art.

Daily Telegraph.

II. FOREIGNERS IN JAPAN.

Some time ago it was known that the Government of Japan had issued an edict, commanding that all foreigners should be forthwith excluded or expelled from all parts of the Empire. To carry out this arbitrary edict it was seen that force might be requisite. The aid of the great lords of the empire, the Daimios, seems therefore to have been claimed. But these feudatories of the Empire appear to have in their turn claimed that the act of the Government should be submitted for their assent. A great Council of Daimios was therefore held, in which it was decided by a majority that the foreigners should *not* be thrust out of the Empire by force. Too little is known of the institutions of Japan to make it clear whether or how far this decision of the Council bound the minority, among whom were some determined and powerful anti-foreigners, the Princes of Satsuma and Nagato for instance. But the minority, whether from usage, or policy, or fear, seems to have for the time, or in appearance, bowed to the will of the majority; and the consequence was a change in the tactics of the exclusionists. The edict of expulsion was withdrawn; but in lieu of it other and not less arbitrary and unjust demands have been made on the foreigners.

Scotsman.

III. BIRTH OF A PRINCE.

The birth of an Heir to the Throne in the second degree places before the mind in one group three Sovereigns, who may not improbably span a whole century in their reigns, and a much longer period in their lives. How much a century is in the history of nations, and what changes there may be between the birth or the accession of the grandfather and the death of the grandchild, we may see by reviewing the interval between the battle of Bosworth and the death of Elizabeth, or the reigns of the first three Edwards. Indeed, when it is remembered that a hundred and twenty-eight years have passed since the birth of Her Majesty's grandfather, and more than a century since his accession, we seem to have before us one of those vast horizons which comprise not only national events but continental re-arrangements, and even the grander revolutions of opinion and sentiment. Though the eyes of most among us are cast far over many a field of battle fought or impending, the time may come when this event of the day, as it seems, may be reverted to as the starting-point of a momentous period and the beginning of a new reach of history. *Times,* Jan. 11, 1864.

IV. THE WRONGS OF THE STOMACH.

Some one has said that if all a man eats in a day were placed upon a dish before him, he would wonder how, after such consumption, he could live and not die. Others put the matter more truly, and tell the " good liver " that he is daily killing himself; not feeding his body, but starving it; filling his blood with the seeds of disease; preparing the way for a short life and a miserable one. Here is a young man of five-and-twenty, a model of strength and activity, brimful of energy and elasticity. Twenty years pass over his head, and the fine muscle has degenerated into fat. He has become corpulent, bloated about the face, wheezy in the chest; complains of indigestion; feels the premonitions of gout in slight quivering pains in the toes and feet, or the creeping stiffness which shows that rheumatism is on its way to console the evening of his life. That is not the effect of time. Look at that sprightly old gentleman, a little shrivelled, it is true, but erect, and still light upon his feet, who walks in and out to business every day from Clapham. He is between sixty and seventy, and tells you he has never had a day's illness in his life. What has been the difference between the two men which has produced such opposite results?

In ninety-nine cases out of a hundred, it is not a difference of constitution, but of habit. The spare, active old man has been a spare eater, a moderate consumer of stimulants. He has been a reasonable master to his stomach. He has known how properly to value a willing servant, and has not overburdened it. He has not taxed the *vis medicatrix naturæ* to get him out of unnecessary hobbles, but has kept clear of them by regular habits, light eating and drinking, and wholesome exercise. Read all this backwards, and you see how the gentleman at forty-five has brought himself to the corpulency of a prize ox, and seems so bursting all over that you are afraid to see him cough or laugh, lest he should have a fit of apoplexy. In ten years more you will find him hobbling about his room upon a pair of crutches, a martyr to gout; or if Nature resents his excesses in some other form, you may find that he is crippled with rheumatism or afflicted with paralysis; or that he is a martyr to dyspepsia—sour, morose, a misery to himself and to every one obliged to be near him. He has over-eaten himself, or wasted the powers of his stomach by excessive stimulants.

V. WRONGS OF THE STOMACH—*continued*.

To pass from a particular instance to the community at large, it is now well ascertained that most of us eat twice as much as we need, and that ninety out of a hundred diseases are of our own making. The gentlemen who whirl about all day in their carriages as if they were rushing to put out a fire, passing from house to house to minister to people afflicted with colds, bilious attacks, headaches, nervous complaints, gout, rheumatism, and the majority of the physical ills that afflict humanity, owe their occupation and its profits to the "wrongs of the stomach." People treat that vital member, which prepares in its wonderful laboratory the streams of life that nourish the whole system, as if it was merely a convenient arrangement for the gratification of the palate and the appetite. As a rule, they don't even take the pains to lighten its labour by making their teeth do the rough part of the work, but bolt their food, gobbling away as long as a cubic barley-corn of the stomach is left uncrammed. They convert it into an organ of sensual enjoyment, forgetting that its office is to prepare supplies to repair the hourly waste of the body, and that, as these supplies are healthy or unhealthy, so will the body be.

But the "wrongs of the stomach" do not involve the question of bodily health only. Mind and matter in this world go together. What affects the one affects the other. Between them stands the moral man who shares their health and sickness. The gross indulgence of the body depraves mind and morals. We know what its effects are amongst the poor, and how they are refined, but essentially similar, amongst the rich. It is not always so, but a healthy man will generally be a better man —abler in mind, more strict in morals, and always a better-tempered man—than the victim of over-eating. Read upon this subject Mr. Lionel Beale's admirable lectures on the "Stomach Medically and Morally Considered," and see what he says upon this vice. Parents especially should ponder over his truths. Some out of love overload their children's stomachs; some out of ignorance or negligence allow them to overload them themselves. Thence comes much of the mortality of early life, and thence certainly comes the habit in after years, when all parental control is gone, of unlimited indulgence. But why should not the stomach be educated as well as the mind; or why should we not say, "Train up the appetite in the way that it should go, and when it is old it will not depart from it"?—*London Review.*

VI. LORD PALMERSTON ON REFORM.

The following are the remarks made by Lord Palmerston in the House of Commons on Mr. Locke King's motion for the second reading of the County Franchise Bill:—"I cannot vote against the bill of my hon. friend, because that might warrant the supposition that I am indisposed to any change in the county franchise. Undoubtedly I am of opinion that there might be an advantageous change effected. At the same time, it is but fair and candid to my hon. friend and to the House to say that I could not vote for the £10 franchise proposed by the Bill. It appears to me that the object we ought all to have in view is to see that all interests in the country are fairly represented. The two leading interests of this country are, on the one hand, the trading and the commercial interests, and, on the other, the agricultural interest, and any alteration of our system which tends to introduce too largely the trading and commercial, or the town element into the agricultural, or country element, would, I think, injuriously disturb the balance which it is essential for the interests of the country that we should maintain. That is the view which I take of the measure of my hon. friend, and therefore, if it should go into committee, I shall not be prepared to vote for the particular franchise which he proposes to introduce. It will be time enough when we are in committee to consider what the franchise should be.

Now, sir, I venture to differ from my hon. friend as to the expediency of the course which he has determined to pursue. It is quite natural that, having fixed his mind upon his particular measure, he should take every fair opportunity of bringing it under the consideration of the House. But I think it would have been better if he had abstained from mooting the question. It is plain to every man, I think, who attends at all to the indications of public opinion in this House and in the country, that there does not exist at the present moment, in this House or out of it, the same interest in such changes as existed some short period since. The fact is that organic changes have been looked to not as a mere end so much as a means. They were looked to as a means of effecting great alterations and improvements in our internal system, our commercial system, our laws, procedure, and other matters. Many of those improvements have been made. Commerce has been freed from its enshacklements, industry has been encouraged by liberty, and many of those alterations and improvements which were to be the result of organic changes have been accomplished by the Legislature as it stands, and therefore there is a less ardent desire for change than existed before those improvements were made. There are also other considerations connected with external affairs, which have tended to allay the desire for organic changes, arising from the events which have occurred in other countries, and which are attributable in a great measure to the influence of organic changes in those countries."

VII. MINISTERIAL CHANGES.

The retirement of the Duke of Newcastle from the Government in consequence of illness will have caused general regret. No minister has been more thoroughly respected and trusted, although the office which he has administered for several years has furnished comparatively few occasions for Parliamentary discussion. Although he is still in middle life, the Duke of Newcastle has had long experience in public affairs. He held two or three offices under Sir Robert Peel, and at last occupied a seat in his Cabinet. During Lord John Russell's Administration he was a prominent member of the small but powerful party which often held the balance of power. As a member of Lord Aberdeen's Government, he was Secretary for the Colonies until the War Office was erected into a separate department, and he has now for nearly five years been again Colonial Minister. When he attended the Prince of Wales to Canada and the United States as his official adviser, the Duke of Newcastle gave universal satisfaction by his discretion and dignity.

VIII. MINISTERIAL CHANGES—*continued*.

The prejudice which at first attached to his administration of the War-Office in 1854 has been long since dissipated by fuller knowledge of the circumstances. In his earnest desire to prosecute the war with effect he stood almost alone among his colleagues. The disasters of the Crimea represented the military organization of a long and careless peace, and the subsequent restoration of efficiency was in no small degree due to the exertions of the Minister who had in the meantime become a sacrifice to popular discontent. The genuine interest which the Duke of Newcastle felt in the national cause was shown by the immediate employment of his compulsory leisure in a visit to the seat of war. No chief of a great patrician house has more uniformly despised the temptation of abandoning himself to the luxury of idleness, and his well-deserved reputation for industry, for vigour, and for honesty has undoubtedly added strength to the Ministry. In political opinion, the Duke of Newcastle has inclined rather to the more Liberal section of the Cabinet than to the prudent Conservatism of Lord Palmerston.

IX. MINISTERIAL CHANGES—*continued*.

In becoming Chancellor of the Duchy, Lord Clarendon perhaps less distinctly waives his higher pretensions than if he had accepted an efficient though subordinate office. As one of the most trusted and experienced members of the dominant party, he would naturally have been included in the Cabinet from its formation if the crowd of claimants had been less urgent. Having for several years administered the Foreign Office, he was probably disinclined to accept any less dignified and conspicuous post, and yet it was impossible to dispute Lord Russell's right to the second place in the Government. Lord Clarendon is one of a fortunate class which is seldom out of office, and he might at one time, if he had wished to transfer his services, have changed his party without sacrificing his official rank. A thoroughly accomplished man of the world, he had considerable practice in diplomacy before he entered Lord Melbourne's Cabinet five-and-twenty years ago. During Lord John Russell's Administration he was Lord-Lieutenant of Ireland, and when Lord Palmerston, under Lord Aberdeen, stepped aside for a time into the obscurity of the Home Office, Lord Clarendon became, after a short interval, Foreign Secretary. He was thought to have shown so much ability in conducting the Russian Correspondence that Lord Derby, when he attempted to form a Government at the beginning of 1855, invited him to continue in the same office. At the close of the war, Lord Clarendon, in conformity with precedent, acted as Plenipotentiary in the Congress of Paris, where he committed the remarkable error of adopting the French language of complaint against the freedom of the Belgian press. His principal defect as a Minister is perhaps an absence of instinctive sympathy with the national opinion or feeling. Diplomatists by profession and by nature are almost always too cosmopolitan to exercise commanding influence at home. *Saturday Review.*

X. THE LAST THIRTEEN YEARS.

Few persons in 1851 could ever have anticipated that the years immediately following the great commemoration of peace would be the prelude to not only the realities but even the technicalities of war. Yet the Great Exhibition had scarcely disappeared when the encampment at Chobham was formed, and that military display was at once succeeded by the campaigns of a great war and the stories of a desperate struggle. Then came the battles in Lombardy, and now the only great Power which had remained at peace has once more drawn its sword against an enemy. Prussia escaped the Crimean and Italian wars only to find herself, as it were, with an obligation to show in Denmark that she, too, had preserved her military capacities, and could enter the lists again if she pleased. But the result has been that war has formed the staple of current history. England, France, Russia, Austria, Prussia, Spain, and the United States have all gone to war, and the stories of their campaigns have furnished the chief subjects of public interest. When the siege of Sebastopol first commenced it was necessary to explain to the public the general character and course of operations which for a quarter of a century had been unknown in Europe, but now every reader is familiar with the successive stages and most technical details of such enterprises. The letters of our two correspondents from the opposing camps at Dybböl have kept the public acquainted with every incident of the siege, and have enabled us to measure the progress of the assailants and the prospects of the garrison as accurately as the engineers on the ground. For the last fortnight everybody could tell you exactly to what point the approaches of the Prussians had been carried, how many guns they had in battery, and how many shells they had thrown on any particular day. The gradual discouragement of the Danes had been pictured with equal fidelity, and we could watch the inevitable exhaustion of their overmatched and outnumbered battalions. The spectacle acquired a painful interest from this disproportion of means. Even with the aid of artificial defences the Danes were no fair match for the Prussians. It was known they must yield, and that the question was one of time alone.—*Times*, April 21, 1864.

THIRD PART.

FORMS OF LETTERS.

(*Official Letter.*)

WESTWARD NATIONAL SCHOOL,
PEYTON, YORKSHIRE, 15*th* Oct. 1864.

SIR,

I have the honour to inform you that the Managers of the above school have appointed as principal teacher Mr. George Ross, late student at the Somerset Training College, where he was classed in the —— division of the second year.

The Managers desire this school to obtain the benefit of the Parliamentary Grant for Education under the provisions of the Revised Code from this date. I await your instructions; and I have the honour to be,

SIR,
Your most obedt. Servant,
EDWARD JACKSON,
Vicar of Westward,
Correspondent for the Managers of
Westward National School.

To the Secretary, Committee of
Privy Council on Education.

(*Official Letter.*)

WHITEHALL, LONDON, S.W.,
11*th* October 1864.

SIR,

I am directed by His Grace the Duke of N. to request you to furnish him with an exact statement of the details of the incident which recently took place in your neighbourhood, and which has called forth so much animadversion from the public press.

You will be good enough to lose no time in complying with his Grace's wishes. I have the honour to be,

SIR,
Your most obedt. servant,
GEORGE WETHERBY.

To HENRY HATFIELD, Esq., J.P.

(*Official Letter.*)

NEWTON, HERTFORDSHIRE,
14*th October* 1864.

SIR,
I have the honour to acknowledge receipt of your letter of the 11th October, in which you inform me that his Grace the Duke of N. "requests an exact statement of the details of the incident which recently took place in this neighbourhood, and which has called forth so much animadversion from the public press," and further requesting me "to lose no time in complying with the request."

Presuming that the incident to which you refer is that commonly headed in the newspapers the "Grange Road Mystery," I took immediate steps for obtaining accurate information on the facts of that case. These facts, in so far as they could be ascertained by me, are enclosed under cover with this letter, and are headed:

MEMORANDUM respecting the incident which took place in the parish of Newton, on or about the 2d October 1863, commonly spoken of as the "Grange Road Mystery."

To that Memorandum I now have the honour respectfully to refer his Grace.

I have the honour to be,
SIR,
Your most obedt. servt.,
HENRY HATFIELD, J.P.

To GEORGE WETHERBY, Esq.

(*Application for a situation as Nurse.*)

EALING, *September* 15, 1864.

MADAM,
I have been told that the place of head nursemaid is vacant in your family. I have had great experience as a nurse, and can be trusted to wash and dress children, to attend to them in sickness, and to make and

mend their clothes. I beg leave respectfully to apply for the place in your family, and to enclose copies of my certificates of character from former mistresses. I can refer you to Mrs. Brunton, Surrey Villa, Camberwell, in whose family I have been for three years and a half.

    I am,
      MADAM,
       Your very obedient servant,
         HANNAH MORE.

MRS. EASTWOOD.

(Application for the situation of Gardener.)

        HEFFORTH, CUMBERLAND,
SIR,   *21st May* 1864.

  I understand that you are in want of a gardener. I was brought up to the work in Scotland, and left my place with a very good character. I enclose a certificate from the master whom I last served, which will show that my character has always been good, and that I understand the management of fruit and flower, as well as vegetable gardens. I have been accustomed to manage forcing-houses.

    I am,
      SIR,
       Your very obedt. servant,
         JOHN MACKINTOSH.

To SIR GEORGE WARREN, Bart.

(Application for the situation of Clerk.)

       WEDGEWOOD, STAFFORDSHIRE,
SIR,   *March* 27, 1864.

  I learn from an advertisement that you have a vacant clerkship in your establishment at present. I beg leave respectfully to request that you would accept me as a candidate for the post, and examine the testimonials which I enclose. The Rev. Mr. Williams, the clergyman whose church I attend, has given me a certificate of character, and has also given me permission to refer you to him for any further information regarding me which you may wish to have. The teacher whose school I last attended has kindly stated in his certificate the progress I made under him in arithmetic and other subjects taught in his school. This letter is in my own handwriting.

I shall be happy to wait upon you, should you wish to see me before deciding on my fitness. As I have never yet had any business appointment, I shall be happy to accept whatever salary you may consider enough for one who has to learn his duties.

I am,
SIR,
Your very obedt. servant,
JOHN NELSON.

To WILLIAM ELWOOD, Esq.

(*Letter from one wishing to emigrate.*)

PLOCTON, DORSETSHIRE,
April 4, 1863.

SIR,
I am a labouring man on the farm of Eatly in this parish. I have a wife and five children, and I wish to emigrate to Australia, as I hear that I can get, both for myself and my children, a better livelihood there than in the old country. Will you be kind enough to tell me what I am to do, and how much it will cost me altogether to take my family to the colony.

I have the honour to be,
SIR,
Your mo. obedt. humble servant,
WILLIAM HODGSON.

To the Secretary
to the Emigration Commissioners.

(*Letter accepting a Situation.*)

NORTON, RUTLAND,
August 16, 1864.

SIR,

I have the honour to acknowledge the receipt of your kind letter of the 15th August, telling me that you have appointed me to the situation of gamekeeper. I beg leave respectfully to thank you for the favour you have done me, and to assure you that I shall always do my best to deserve the continuance of your good opinion.

I am,

SIR,

Your obedt. humble servant,

JAMES S. LAWSON.

(*Note of Invitation.*)

Mr. and Mrs. Brown present their compliments to Mr. and Mrs. Williams, and request the pleasure (or honour) of their company at dinner on Saturday,[1] the 7th September, at six o'clock.

22, BRIXTON SQUARE, LONDON,
August 31, 1864.

(*Note of Acceptance.*)

Mr. and Mrs. Williams will have much pleasure in dining with Mr. and Mrs. Brown on Saturday, the 7th September, at six o'clock.

15, HIGHBURY TERRACE, LONDON,
Septr. 1, 1864.

---

[1] If it is an evening party, then write, " company on the evening of 7th September, at nine (or ten) o'clock."

FORMS OF LETTERS.

(Business Note.)

18, River Street, London,
Nov. 5, 1864.

To Messrs. Truman and Wye.

Gentlemen,
Have the goodness to forward to us at your earliest convenience one bale of cotton, and charge the same to our account.

We are,
Gentlemen,
Your obedient servants,
Hanbury and Ross.

(Reply.)

8, Water St., Liverpool,
Nov. 7, 1864.

To Messrs. Hanbury and Ross.

Gentlemen,
We beg leave to acknowledge receipt of your favour of the 5th Nov., and have to-day forwarded, per goods-train, the bale of cotton, as ordered by you, and we have charged the same to your account. The invoice is enclosed. Waiting further orders,

We are,
Gentlemen,
Your obedt. servants,
Truman and Wye.

DIRECTIONS AS TO MODES OF ADDRESSING OTHERS IN WRITING.

(1.) In writing to a gentleman, knight, baronet, or lady, always address, "Sir," or "Madam," and conclude, "I have the honour to be, Sir (or Madam), your most obedt. servant."

(2.) If the lady you are addressing is the wife of a knight, baronet, or baron, conclude,
I have the honour to be,
Madam,
Your ladyship's most obedt. servant,
T. C.
and in the body of the letter use the words "your ladyship," instead of the word "you."

(3.) In addressing barons, viscounts, earls, and marquises, begin, "My lord," and conclude, "I have the honour to be,
My lord,
(If a marquis, 'My lord marquis')
Your obedt. humble servant,
A. B."

(In the body of the letter, say "your lordship" instead of "you.")
The superscription should be, if to a baron,
To Lord ——.

If to a viscount,
To the Right Hon.
Viscount B——.

If to an earl,
To the Right Hon.
Earl C——.

If to a marquis,
To the most Honourable
The Marquis of D——.

(4.) In addressing a duke, begin,
"My Lord Duke."
(In the body of the letter say "your Grace" instead of "you.")
Conclude,
I have the honour to be,
My Lord Duke,
Your Grace's most obedt. servant,
G. W.

N.B.—Viceroys and Governors of colonies are addressed as "Your Excellency."

Clerical Addresses.

(Bishop.) "My Lord Bishop."
Address as "Your Lordship," and superscribe,
To the Right Rev.
The Lord Bishop of ——.

(Archbishop.) "My Lord Archbishop."
Concluding,
I have the honour to be,
My Lord Archbishop,
Your Grace's most obedt. servant,
T. L.

Superscribe,
To His Grace
The Archbishop of ——.

(Dean.) Superscribe,
To the very Rev.
The Dean of ——.

(Archdeacon.) Superscribe,
          To the Venerable
                    The Archdeacon of ———.
Clergymen not dignitaries, as well as Deans and Archdeacons, are addressed, "Reverend Sir."

"Right Honourable" is prefixed to the designations of all above the rank of earls' eldest sons and Privy Councillors.

MISCELLANEOUS EXERCISES ON SPELLING,

BEING THE WORDS MIS-SPELT BY CANDIDATES FOR CIVIL SERVICE APPOINTMENTS.

acquiescence	abstinence	advisable	cathedral
assassination	apology	acquainted	cavaliers
ability	assembled	aid	cavalry
aspen	arithmetic	accountant	celebrated
acclamations	appointed	arguing	censures
accounts	accompanied	accomplices	champion
arbitrary	acme	annually	character
accuracy	acquitted	animated	cheerfulness
annulled	asserting	aquiline	chieftains
ambassador	adjacent	besiege	chronicles
approached	augur	behaviour	circumstance
appreciate	apprehension	baptized	civilisation
apprentice	anxious	business	clapped
adequately	agreement	blockade	clerk
ambitious	abbey	brilliant	cloisters
amiability	apartment	beginning	coalition
Archipelago	adultery	barbarous	colleagues
admirably	adulation	burgesses	collision
anomalous	animosities	barrels	committed
authority	accusation	buried	committee
ascended	author	buoyant	commonalty
appalling	arranging	bowels	comparative
agreeable	archives	bloodiest	compelled
allegiance	administered	banished	competent
abhorred	avaricious	capacious	complacent
aggression	alacrity	caprice	complaisant
allowance	anticipated	career	completely
allege	anonymous	catastrophe	complexion

concealment	degradation	entertainment	finances
conceived	Deity	exaggerations	flagellation
concluded	deliberations	every	fain
condescend	deliverance	earnest	forest
condign	derived	encouraging	fascinating
condition	describe	extremities	ferocity
confederacies	designs	enormous	federal
conferred	desiring	especially	finally
confidence	desolation	expedient	fundamental
conqueror	dissolution	evening	furlong
conscience	dissolved	executing	family
consequence	desponding	expenses	further
considerable	desperate	expressed	fulfil
consistent	despotism	enticing	fervour
conspicuous	diligent	empowered	facility
conspirator	disagreeable	enacting	feigned
constitute	disappointing	eminence	grandeur
consummate	discerned	eminently	grievances
continually	discipline	establishing	guardian
contractors	discretion	eligible	gaoler
contrary	discussed	exercising	genealogists
control	disorderly	early	guidance
convenience	displayed	expectation	government
corpse	distinguished	endeavour	geographically
correspondent	dissatisfaction	enrolled	heptarchy
corruptible	dissent	exotics	horizon
countenance	dissipating	eighth	hostess
counties	distinction	exhausted	hierarchy
courageous	duchies	extirpate	hostages
courtesy	ecclesiastical	economy	hypocrite
credulity	enthusiasm	existence	humane
crisis	embraced	enemies	human
criticism	elements	efficacy	hereditary
decent	etiquette	extraordinary	heroic
deceit	enveloped	excellent	inoperative
decreed	ensued	evident	intercourse
deficiencies	emancipated	earthenware	inestimable
definitely	emolument	foreign	illustrious

MISCELLANEOUS EXERCISES ON SPELLING.

irresistible	independence	mizen	ordinary
indecision	inseparably	mission	official
implacable	intermixed	material	offences
inevitably	jealous	ministers	owner
insurrections	joyous	minstrels	opportunity
integrity	jewellery	menacing	operate
irreproachable	knowledge	mere	orders
irreparable	knocked	mercy	occurred
improvement	knew	military	opposite
inconvenience	leisure	militia	own
impetuous	labourers	making	opposition
intellectual	lie	mead	origin
intelligence	linen	muzzle	ornament
interfered	liberties	mulattoes	obliged
increased	losses	magazines	ocean
intricate	liveliness	monarchs	pretensions
island	laborious	miserable	powerful
incorrigible	legate	mechanically	prize
idolaters	language	machinery	position
insensibly	licentiousness	maddened	prevailed
impostor	mountains	mean	parricide
inordinate	melancholy	measure	patiently
industrious	memorial	martyr	prorogued
indebted	memorable	mathematics	possess
immigrant	moral	mightiest	particularly
ignorance	myrtle	manifested	partiality
imbecile	mansion	minority	precipitately
inscriptions	mastiff	monks	period
imaginary	magnanimity	mouldering	perpetually
innocent	mentioned	merchandise	priest
innocence	mortgaging	might	postponing
incendiaries	manuring	massacre	pernicious
illiterate	managing	neighbour	peaceably
imperceptible	misfortune	nourishment	Parliament
innumerable	malcontents	narrative	pitied
indispensable	moderated	noisy	prepossessed
immediately	maze	nauseous	preparatory
inconsistent	martial	non-existence	practise

MISCELLANEOUS EXERCISES ON SPELLING.

practice	reverence	scheme	travellers
practicable	receive	stoically	traitors
practically	relieved	subjects	threw
philosophy	reassemble	sufficiently	tendency
prebendaries	rudiments	successive	tense
persuasion	rigour	stratagem	usurper
panegyrics	rode	stretch	unanimous
parallels	ridiculous	shield	unfortunate
politician	renowned	scruples	unfledged
privileges	reins	style	undoubtedly
presidencies	review	symmetry	unsuitable
plainness	symptoms	satire	universities
proselytes	sovereign	swayed	unscrupulous
punctilious	swept	scarcely	unskilfully
prophet	signature	separate	usually
privacy	sojourned	shepherd	vexatious
perceive	species	superiority	vigilance
prejudices	slaughtered	several	victorious
pursue	secretaries	sacrificed	vengeance
promiscuous	surgeon	suspicion	violent
perilous	system	second	volumes
precipices	sincerely	sour	villain
people	soul	successful	vats
prayers	susceptibility	stolidly	vizier
poems	sepulchre	subduing	village
pamphlet	surrendered	suggested	where
quarrels	solicitor	scarcely	waned
qualities	sheriff	serious	wear
really	saltpetre	tenacious	warmth
regiments	shrewd	tyrant	whirlwind
revenue	salaries	tomb	women
requisites	seized	terrible	wives
reign	shipping	their	worse
recommend	superstition	twilight	woollen
readily	straits	tranquillity	wharves
right	specie	traffic	yielding
recesses	scene	tacit	

LATIN AND FRENCH PHRASES IN COMMON USE.

Ab initio, from the beginning.
Ad finem, to the end.
Ad hominem, pertaining to the man.
Ad infinitum, without limit.
Ad libitum, at pleasure.
Ad valorem, according to value.
Alias, otherwise.
Alibi, elsewhere; proof of having been elsewhere.
Alma mater, a cherishing mother.
Anglicè, in English.
Anno Domini, in the year of our Lord.
Audi alteram partem, Hear the other side.
Bona fide, in good faith.
Cacoëthes scribendi, an itch for writing.
Cæteris paribus, other things being equal.
Compos mentis, of a sound mind.
Cornu copiæ, the horn of plenty.
Cui bono, to what good purpose?
Dei gratia, by the grace of God.
De facto, in fact; in deed.
De jure, by right or law.
De novo, over again; anew.
Dramatis personæ, actors representing the characters in a play.

E pluribus unum, one formed of many. [The motto of the United States.]
Ergo, therefore.
Excelsior, loftier.
Ex officio, by virtue of office.
Ex parte, on one side.
Exit, he goes out.
Facsimile, a close imitation.
Habeas corpus, you may have the body.
Hic jacet, here he lies.
Incognito, unknown; disguised.
In forma pauperis, as a pauper.
In limine, at the outset.
In propria persona, in his own person.
In statu quo, in the same state.
In terrorem, as a warning.
In toto, altogether.
Ipse dixit, he himself said it; an assertion.
Ipso facto, by the fact itself.
Lapsus linguæ, a slip of the tongue.
Literatim, letter for letter.
Lusus naturæ, a freak of nature.
Magna Charta, the great charter.
Malum per se, an evil of itself.
Mala fide, in bad faith

Maximum, the greatest.
Memento mori, be mindful of death.
Minimum, the smallest.
Mirabile dictu, wonderful to tell.
Modus operandi, mode of operating.
Multum in parvo, much in a little.
Nem. con., no one opposing; unanimously.
Ne plus ultra, the utmost extent.
Ne quid nimis, nothing in excess.
Nolens volens, unwilling or willing.
Nisi prius, unless before.
Passim, everywhere.
Per annum, by the year.
Per diem, by the day.
Per se, by itself.
Post mortem, after death.
Prima facie, on the first appearance.
Pro bono publico, for the public good.
Pro et con, for and against.
Pro re nata, for the occasion.
Pro tempore (*Pro tem.*), for the time.
Quam primum, immediately.
Quantum, how much.
Quantum sufficit, sufficient quantity.
Quid pro quo, something for something.
Quondam, formerly.
Requiescat in pace, may he rest in peace.
Sanctum sanctorum, the Holy of Holies.
Secundem artem, according to art.
Sine die, without day specified.
Sine qua non, that which is indispensable.
Suaviter in modo, gently in manner.
Summum bonum, the chief good.
Te Deum, a hymn of thanksgiving.
Terra firma, solid earth.
Una voce, with one voice.
Ultra, beyond; excessive.
Veni, Vidi, Vici, I came, I saw, I conquered.
Versus, against.
Via, by the way of.
Vice versa, the terms being exchanged.
Viva voce, with the living voice.
Vide, see.
Vox populi, the voice of the people.
Beau monde, the gay world.
Bon mot, a lively phrase; a jest.
Cap-à-pie, from head to foot.
En masse, all together.
Mêlée, a conflict; a fight.
Nonchalance, indifference.
Sang froid, coolness; unconcern.
Soirée, an evening entertainment.
Sans souci, without care or anxiety.
Vivat Regina, long live the Queen.

www.ingramcontent.com/pod-product-compliance
Lightning Source LLC
Chambersburg PA
CBHW020113170426
43199CB00009B/511